T0115668

Big Bucks!

Books by Ken Blanchard and Sheldon Bowles

GUNG HO!

RAVING FANS

Big Bucks!

Ken Blanchard / Sheldon Bowles

WILLIAM MORROW

An Imprint of HarperCollins*Publishers*

HarperCollins books may be purchased for educational, business, or sales promotional use. For information please write: Special Markets Department, HarperCollins Publishers Inc., 10 East 53rd Street, New York, NY 10022.

Printed on acid-free paper

Designed by Nancy Singer Olaguera

Library of Congress Cataloging-in-Publication Data has been applied for.

ISBN 0-688-17035-8

12 13 14 BP 10 9 8 7 6 5 4 3 2

Dedicated to

our colleagues and friends
from

THE YOUNG PRESIDENTS' ORGANIZATION (YPO)

including
those who have "graduated" to

WORLD PRESIDENTS' ORGANIZATION (WPO)

and

CHIEF EXECUTIVES' ORGANIZATION (CEO)

who helped and encouraged
us over the years to be the
best that we could be

INTRODUCTION

Big Bucks! completes our trilogy which describes the three key factors that determine the long-term success and effectiveness of an organization: as a provider of choice (*Raving Fans*), as an employer of choice (*Gung Ho!*), and as an investment of choice (*Big Bucks!*).

We like to think of these three factors—often called "the triple bottom line"—as the legs of a three-legged stool. We like the analogy because to stand, the stool needs all three legs. Take one leg away and the stool falls down. Or if one leg is rotten or weak, it will eventually break with disastrous consequences. Each leg is equally important and vital.

We started our trilogy with *Raving Fans* because in today's world taking care of your customers is no longer an option. Customers are more sophisticated than ever and if they're not treated well they go elsewhere.

Readers of *Raving Fans* were taken by the idea that *satisfying* customers just isn't good enough—you have to treat them so well that they want to brag about you. But people said to us, "How can you create Raving Fan Service® with employees who feel unappreciated and therefore are unmotivated?" That's when we decided to write *Gung Ho!* and attempt to teach managers how to develop a totally committed and motivated staff.

Writing *Big Bucks!* last was no accident. We believe people often get it backward. They want to make more money, increase profits, so they concentrate attention on the financial numbers rather than the *people* who are customers and the *people* who look after the customers, the staff. The best definition of profit we have ever heard is: *Profit is the applause you get for taking care of your customers and creating a motivating environment for your people*. Thus, the triple bottom line.

The secrets or tests for moneymaking described in *Big Bucks!* work both for people individually as well as for managers trying to make money for their department or organization. We hope you enjoy the story of Len, the young man searching for the secrets to moneymaking, and his adventures with Rabbi Silver, Father Murphy, Pastor Edwards, and the moneymakers from their congregations. With the completion of this book we feel that managers will have the necessary knowledge to be successful. After all, it takes gung-ho people to create raving fan customers who make your cash register go *ka-ching, ka-ching, ka-ching* with big bucks. Good luck!

Ken Blanchard and Sheldon Bowles

CONFUSION CORNER

Len had two pair: jacks and sevens. Not much, but his best hand so far.

"I'll see you," he said as he slid five pennies forward.

"What you got?" asked Rabbi Silver, turning over a pair of queens and two aces.

The old boiler picked that moment, as it did every five minutes or so, to emit a mighty clunk and wheeze. Len had got used to the boiler, but not the poker game to which the rabbi had invited him. Len and the rabbi had met for the first time the previous evening. It was a toss-up who had been more surprised. Len, finding himself in a synagogue, or the rabbi, discovering an early arrival for Shabbat service down on his knees praying!

Sensing Len's distress, the rabbi had eased himself into a nearby pew. As Len stood up to go, the rabbi said hello.

2

"Hello, Father," Len replied.

"Actually, it's Rabbi, except when I'm home, then sometimes it's father, but more often I'm just 'the old man,' " said the rabbi with a gentle laugh.

"Oh, sorry," said Len, looking around the dimly lit sanctuary. "I thought this was St. Mary's."

"Across the road. But don't worry. We share parking lots at Christmas and on High Holy days. You're always welcome here."

The synagogue didn't have a confession box, but within minutes Len found himself telling his troubles to the rabbi. This, in turn, had led to an invitation to the card game.

"Please come. Tomorrow night. Side door. St. Mary's, eight o'clock. I think you'll find it a help."

Rabbi Silver, Father Murphy, Pastor Edwards, and Len started with 100 pennies each. When the game ended, all 400 pennies would be gathered up and put away until the following week. How, Len wondered, could this penny-ante card game, with *returnable* pennies, help his problem: money. To be specific, how to make more money—lots more money, big money.

The intersection of Elm Street and Lonsdale Avenue was known as Confusion Corner. Beth El Synagogue, St. Mary's, and the Evangelical Church of the Book occupied three corners. On the fourth stood the Lonsdale Market Inn, a sleazy hotel known for its hard-drinking bar and harder clientele.

The question was, Which of the four corners held man's best hope? That was confusing enough. Just what this poker game had to do with Len's problem was even more confusing.

The night before he'd gone for a walk to think things over. He felt guilty about not being a better provider at home. Here it was June, and that evening his wife, Linda, had written the check to pay off their final Christmas bill. Worse, he knew that their vow to build a nest egg for next Christmas wasn't going to happen. Taxes, mortgage payments, dentist bills, Linda's parking spot at work, dry cleaning, gas and electric bills . . . Well, it went out as fast, or faster, than it came in. It was a life he was determined to change. Len didn't just want more money. He wanted to be rich. Then he smiled and said to himself, "Filthy rich."

Not knowing where to turn for advice, Len had ended up on his knees in what he thought was St. Mary's Church. Maybe a divine intervention was his only chance for help.

One thing he was sure of, he wasn't going to get rich playing cards. The evening was young and he was already down to 65 cents.

"So you want to make money?" said Pastor Edwards unexpectedly as he expertly flicked the cards to each player.

"Lots of money. Len's interested in big bucks," said the rabbi.

"You've come to the right place," said Father Murphy, giving Len a warm smile before scooping up his cards.

"Here's how it works. Some years ago, when the three of us started to meet, we decided that if we pooled our resources we could accomplish more for God than if we didn't. We started with the easy things like parking and pianos, but soon found the largest and best resource we had to share was our congregations."

"Which brings us to money," said Rabbi Silver. "We realized we had special people in our congregations with significant skills. We had great negotiators, mediators, motivators; people who could really help others."

"And as we looked at our congregations, we realized we had another skilled group: moneymakers," said Father Murphy. "So we approached these people individually and asked two simple questions: Is there a skill set or knowledge base that lets people make big money, and if so, are the skills and knowledge teachable?"

"The answers were clear," said Rabbi Silver. "Our moneymakers all agreed there were such skills and knowledge and also agreed they could be taught! Except that some people never learned. But they said these were exceptions."

"What surprised us," said Pastor Edwards, "was that when we talked to these moneymakers about what it took to make money, their suggestions were very similar. They put their heads together and quickly agreed on a game plan to help others who want to make big bucks."

"What we learned," said Rabbi Silver, "is that to be a big moneymaker you have to pass three tests: The test of joy. The test of purpose. The test of creativity."

"What we're offering you," said Father Murphy solemnly, "is a chance to master these three tests. We each have specialists in our congregations ready to teach one of the secrets. If you choose to accept our offer, Richard Paul of Rabbi Silver's congregation will teach you how to meet the test of joy, Roberta Bains from St. Mary's will guide you through the test of purpose, and finally, Carlos Grover from Church of the Book will prepare you for the test of creativity."

While the three were speaking, the card game had stopped. Now they sat quietly looking at Len, waiting for his reaction. Len, for his part, was stunned. He could hardly believe that these three clergymen, playing cards next to a bad-tempered, asthmatic boiler in a church basement, could really be of any help. Except for one thing, the names: Richard Paul, Roberta Bains, Carlos Grover. Anyone who read the newspapers knew those names. These were enormously successful and wealthy individuals. Until now the only thing Len knew they had in common was that they were self-made multimillionaires.

"Why me?" Len heard himself say.

"We're looking for people to help, whom we like. Rabbi Silver invited you here, as we do with all candidates, for the three of us to check you out. It's amazing how much one can learn about a person's character with just a few hands of poker," said Father Murphy.

"We're told that the secrets to pass the three tests will work for almost anyone, so we want to be sure that our candidates have character," said Rabbi Silver.

"By character we mean people who operate from a set of values," said Father Murphy as he gently fingered his cards in the hope an ace might suddenly appear. "Tell me, why do you want to be rich?"

So many answers flooded Len's mind.

"I want to pay my bills. Feed my family better. Make life easier for my wife, Linda. It would be great if Hanna, our 10-year-old, could take music lessons. And Jimmy, our 12-year-old, wants new hockey skates. The car is falling apart, but if I buy a new one, it just means the monthly payments go up. I don't really want money for expensive things, but I do want to be able to provide properly for my family, get the kids a good education, make sure that if something happened to me Linda would still be okay financially, and stop worrying once and for all that the wolf is just around the corner and ready to arrive at our front door.

"I'm working my head off right now, but nothing seems to change. There's got to be a better way."

"Fair enough," said Pastor Edwards, "but let's suppose you succeed in making lots of money, big money. Is there anything else you'd like to do?"

Len started to reply. "For one thing I'd go up north to fish. I love fishing." Then he stopped. What he was about to say was he'd never shared with anyone else before.

"If I had enough money I'd like to be able to help others in need. It's just a dream. But I'd like to make that dream come true."

"*Ka-ching!*" said Rabbi Silver.

"*Ka-ching?*"

"That's the cash register ringing," said Rabbi Silver. "It also means I'm pleased with your answer to Father Murphy's question. You see, we don't want to help anyone who thinks accumulating wealth is just an end in itself, or someone who thinks the person who dies with the most toys wins."

"Are you saying that money is bad?" asked Len.

"Not at all," said the rabbi. "It can be, but that's only when you put money and wealth on a pedestal and become blind to everything else in life. Money isn't the problem, though. It's your attitude toward what you've got that can be a problem."

"Well, one thing about being in debt," said Len, "I don't have to worry about my attitude toward money."

"Oh, but you do," said Father Murphy.

"If you don't pay attention to significance before you're wealthy, by the time you're a millionaire it may be too late," said Pastor Edwards.

"Significance," Len said tentatively, as if testing out the word.

"That's right, significance," said Rabbi Silver gently. "Success is about worth. Significance is about worthwhile. Success is getting. Significance is giving—giving time, talent, money, and service to others. In the end that's what really matters."

"Charles Dickens illustrated that beautifully with Scrooge in his classic *A Christmas Carol*," interjected Pastor Edwards, "When you die, what you've accomplished financially is often quickly forgotten. What's remembered is what you did for others.

"Our mission is to help our moneymaking students keep things in perspective. So while Richard Paul, Roberta Bains, and Carlos Grover will be your success coaches, we'll make sure you don't forget significance."

The three old friends and Len sat for a moment to consider the importance of what had been said, and then, as if by some unspoken common consent, the card game resumed.

"So what do you say? Are you ready to face the tests of joy, purpose, and creativity?" asked Pastor Edwards.

"Yes. Yes, I am," said Len with enthusiasm.

"That's great," said Rabbi Silver. "Seeing as I introduced you to our moneymaker program, I'll be your chief significance sponsor and keep in touch with you in that aspect of your journey. As for the success side, I took the liberty of checking with Richard Paul to find out when he could meet you. Would Wednesday morning work for you?"

"It would."

"Then let's play cards," said Father Murphy. "I'm having a great night—I'm way ahead."

"Father, you should be doing the tests of joy, purpose, and creativity," said Len with a laugh.

"Sssshh!" went Pastor Edwards. "Character problem," he stage-whispered to Len.

"Judge not, lest ye be judged," replied Father Murphy in his most pious voice.

"Cards, gentlemen, cards," commanded Rabbi Silver.

"Blessed are the peacemakers," Len chimed in.

"Amen," said Rabbi Silver as he placed a two-cent opening bet.

THE TEST OF JOY

Promptly at 9:00 A.M. Wednesday, Richard Paul's secretary ushered Len into her boss's office. Richard stood up from behind his desk and took three easy, fast strides across the room with his hand outstretched. He wore his 68 years with grace. From the full head of perfectly groomed hair to the tassel on his black soft-leather shoes, Richard presented the picture of a wealthy businessman with abundant energy and a taste for elegance.

The office, however, didn't match the man. Len's eyes focused on Richard's desk. It was a large sheet of finished plywood supported at each end by white plastic soft-drink cases.

Len was so surprised he blurted out, "That's an interesting desk you've got there."

"It works well and the price was right," replied Richard with obvious pride. "When I was younger I used to have a very fancy desk."

"What happened?" asked Len.

"It got in the way of making money, so I got rid of it. I'll never forget the day I was sitting at my elegant desk with Ralph, one of my managers. We were comparing actual expenses with our budgeted ones. When I found out how much was being spent on toilet paper, I was upset. I could buy toilet paper at the supermarket at a better price than we were buying it by the case.

"I looked across the desk at Ralph and saw he wasn't as concerned as I was. Right then and there I understood that if I was sitting in a big office behind a fancy desk, it was going to be darn hard for me to complain about how others spent money and expect them to take me seriously. I had a credibility problem."

"So that's how you make money," said Len. "You keep tight control on all expenses no matter how small."

"No, Len," replied Richard. "Expenses are just one issue when it comes to making big money, but Carlos Grover will cover all that with you later. First you have to pass the test of joy. But before we go on, tell me, do you want to make big bucks for yourself or for your company?"

"Both, really," said Len. "My real goal is to make money for myself, but if I could also make big money for my company, that would be wonderful. Does it make a difference?"

"It doesn't. There is a secret to each of the three tests you have to meet. The secrets are essentially the same whether it's personal or corporate, but I always like to find out. It's mostly curiosity, but it helps to know where you're coming from," replied Richard.

"Do I pass?" asked Len.

"You sure do," said Richard. "Now, are you ready?"

"Yes sir, I am."

"Then let's start with an easy question. What's money?"

"Money? Well, it's mostly paper some government says is money. It can also be copper, silver, even gold in some places. A storehouse of value, I guess," ventured Len.

"That's good. What creates the value, then?"

Len took a moment to consider Richard's question. "I'd say it was providing goods or services that someone else needs. Doing something."

"Excellent," replied Richard. "That's the chain. Value is determined by what people say value is, for something they need or want. There's an important distinction here you need to understand. The buyers determine the value, but you create the value. It's a creative process. You hit the nail right on the head when you said, 'Doing something.' "

"So making money is about doing what people value. Doing the right thing. Being in the right business," said Len.

"That's a start all right, but before we talk about that there's another aspect of money I want you to understand. Tell me, how much money is there? If you added it all up?"

"I've no idea. In the whole world there's lots of it. Just not enough of it at my house," said Len with a smile. "More than that I can't tell you."

"All right, then here's a question you *can* answer. How much money can there be at any one time?"

Len was surprised to hear that he should be able to answer that question. He had no idea how much money there could be at any one time.

Richard broke the silence. "Trick question. I can't tell you to the penny either. The answer is that it's limitless."

After he'd given Len a moment to think this over, Richard added, "The bottom line, for your bottom line, is that money can be limitless. The more you create, the more you have to spend or invest, and that leads to others having more to spend or invest."

Then Richard gave Len a life-altering lesson. "What you need to understand is that money is like love. You can always create more love. If a mother has one child, she can give that child all her love. The instant a second child is born she has just as much love for the new one. That's a 100 percent instant increase."

"True," said Len.

"It is true," said Richard. "And one of the great things about love is that the more love there is in a home, the more love gets created. A loving community creates love faster, far faster, than an uncaring one. And for someone to get more love they don't have to steal love from someone else. A five-year-old sometimes has trouble believing it, but a new baby in the house may take a mother's time from the older child, but never her love. Time is finite. Love is not."

"Again you're right," said Len.

"I am," said Richard. "Now here's the lesson: Money is much like love. To have it doesn't necessarily mean you have permanently diminished someone else's pile. Certainly their pile might get smaller for the moment. However, you've created value for them. You've traded them something they can use, either to sustain themselves or to help them create value and earn more money. That, after all, is the proper use for their money, their storehouse of value.

"Remember this. Money, like love, can be created. Money, like love, is limitless. Money, like love, is most easily created where it already exists."

"To make big bucks," said Len with awe, "I don't have to take anyone else's money and leave them deprived. I can create value for them. That leaves them better equipped to create value for someone else. I've never understood that before."

"It really is exciting, isn't it?" said Richard. "There is no limit to wealth. There is no limit to the money you can make. And that's the word, 'make.' It's not 'taking,' it's 'making.' What's really so great, as you've just said, is that the better those around you do, the better you'll do."

"I like it," said Len with a big grin. "I really like it."

"Thought you would," said Richard.

"What I've told you so far is the truth, but it isn't the whole truth," Richard went on. "Creating wealth by creating value is the honest way to make money as far as I'm concerned. But you should be aware that some moneymakers, and some very successful ones at that, become wealthy by skimming money from others, not creating new wealth. Some of these people wind up in jail. Others who may be unethical, but not legally crooks, can even wind up as public heroes."

Len nodded his head in agreement. He could think of a couple of wealthy people who matched Richard's description.

"I think the real creation of money comes from serving others. It's honorable. Creativity is a gift from God, and I believe we honor God when we use His gifts to serve others. When people pervert that, I get upset," said Richard, thumping his fist down on the arm of his chair.

"It's worth being upset about," said Len. "One thing that would bother me about being wealthy is some of the people I'd be lumped with. On the other hand, some of the people in my struggling middle-class bracket aren't so hot either."

"Well then, if your neighbors can be a problem no matter where you live, let's see what we can do about putting you in with the wealthy crowd," Richard said as he started to laugh.

"Suits me," said Len.

"Now we've got that out of the way, let's go back to the formula we discovered earlier: Value is determined by what people will pay for something they want. But you create what they value. It's 'making.' It's 'doing.' And as you said, it's about doing the right thing, doing the right work."

"So what's the right thing?" Len asked.

"I can't tell you what the right thing is for you. But I can tell you how to find out. That's what the test of joy is all about."

From his inside coat pocket Richard took out his wallet. Shuffling through its contents, he picked out a white card, dog-eared and smudged with age.

Len leaned forward, eager to discover some magic formula that would identify the next wave of customer demands and, beyond that, those demands that would yield a high-profit-margin business. He was in for an even bigger surprise.

"I've carried this card with me ever since I learned the three secrets of making money," said Richard. "When I started to work with Roberta Bains and Carlos Grover, I showed it to them. They agreed the wording was succinct and matched their thinking perfectly. You'll find they each have a similar card of their own now.

"I wrote the secret to the first test on one side of the card and the secrets to the second and third tests on the other. The three secrets are powerful, but to many people they're worthless because they can't believe the power of a simple truth."

Richard covered the card with his hand and slid it across the coffee table toward Len, who looked down expectantly.

Before he uncovered the card, Richard said: "This is the first and greatest secret of making money. It is more powerful than any of the others. It's the answer to the test of joy. Unless you meet this test, unless you understand and believe in this secret, you will never make big money." He lifted his hand. Looking down, Len saw written:

The Test of Joy

You Can't Make Money Unless You're Having FUN

Len looked up, wondering if Richard was teasing him. It wasn't what he'd expected. He could see from the look on Richard's face that he was perfectly serious. He looked back down at the card: YOU CAN'T MAKE MONEY UNLESS YOU'RE HAVING FUN.

"I suspect you are beginning to wonder if I've lost a few marbles, right?" asked Richard.

"Well . . ."

"I don't blame you. The first time I was told the secret I couldn't believe it myself. It seemed silly. It will seem silly to you until you live with it and think about it. But if you give it a chance, it will become one of the most profound and powerful truths you'll ever learn."

"I see what you mean about belief," replied Len. "But I confess I don't understand. I've had fun doing a lot of things, but I never made any money having fun. In fact, fun things always seem to cost money. I would have thought your card would read: *You can't make money unless you work hard*. Or something like that."

Richard looked directly at Len and patiently replied, "That's exactly what it says. Clear your mind and listen to me. I'll explain.

"Making money requires an exuberance and an intensity that's impossible to generate or sustain unless you're enjoying yourself enormously. If you aren't really excited about whatever it is you're doing, you can't expect to make big bucks, for yourself or for your company.

"There are thousands of examples. Ray Kroc, who built the McDonald's restaurant chain, could talk for hours about a French fry. When it came to cleanliness, he was a fanatic. This man loved restaurants. Try to imagine Ray Kroc building the business he did, making the money he made, if he wasn't having fun."

"I don't mean to sound like a doubter," said Len, "but if I was making all the money Ray Kroc was making, I think I'd be having a lot of fun, too. And boy could I learn to love restaurants."

"That's not a wrong answer, but it's not a right one either," said Richard. "I'm a great believer that you can find good things, enrichment, even true joy in most any work if you approach it with the right attitude. If you allow yourself to be open to the possibility that your work could be wonderful and then aggressively seek the positive, chances are you'll wind up charmed and enchanted with your work.

"So, yes, you can learn to love work. You can also decide to have fun. But not after you're making money. The fun has to come first. You can't make money unless what you're doing already excites you, and Ray Kroc was excited about his restaurants long before they became big moneymakers. I'm not saying you need to spend every minute laughing and clapping your hands for joy. Sometimes it's a tough grind. But that's in the details. Above all, and despite annoyances and real problems, the business has to be fun. Got it?" asked Richard.

"I think so," replied Len cautiously. "A friend of mine became headmaster of a private school and was very successful at it. I remember thinking, if the school was a business he would have made a fortune. I once asked him how he could work so hard and he said he wasn't working. He said he was just playing. He told me he was like a kid in a candy shop, because every day was so exciting."

"That's it exactly," said Richard. "You can't really expect to make big bucks until you can't tell the difference between work and play. I don't want anybody to work for me. I want them to play with me."

Len thought about what Richard was telling him, and it began to make sense. "Essentially then, what you're saying is if I'm having a good time, then I'll be glad to put in the hours and put out the effort and energy to be a success."

"Right you are," replied Richard. "But it's the effort and the energy that is most important. Long hours don't necessarily translate into big money. It's the intensity of purpose while you're at it—not overtime at the office or at home—that really counts.

"You see," continued Richard, "there is no inherent difference between work and play. They both take mental and physical energy. The difference is in your mind-set. Making a speech can be work for some and play for others. So can analyzing a financial statement or amending a legal document. Some people hate it. Some people love to do it."

"And fun can make money in any business?" asked Len.

"I can't prove it," Richard replied, "but from what I've seen I suspect big bucks can be made in most any business, or for your own pocket, provided you're having fun and you pass the other two tests."

Len took his pen and notebook out of his pocket and jotted down:

FUN
is when WORK
becomes PLAY

Len looked at what he'd written while Richard remained silent. It was a bit of a paradox. He'd always believed that someone who played at business wasn't going to be successful. But now he was being told success could only come to those who went to work to play. And they were playing because they were having fun. In fact, they had so much fun they didn't think of it as work at all.

On top of that, Richard had told him that most any business could be a good financial success if the people in it were having fun and knew how to pass the other two tests. Len had always assumed that the most important element of success was being in the right business at the right time.

"I wonder if you could tell me more about your idea that any business can make big money?" asked Len.

"Sure. Let me give you an example," said Richard. "Let's go back to McDonald's. I guess you'd tell me that it was obvious that McDonald's would be a success, it was a sure winner right from the beginning?"

"Yes. I'd say it was a predictable winner from day one," replied Len. "I hope you're not going to tell me that McDonald's was a business not likely to succeed?"

"You know, Len, McDonald's hasn't always been around. I'm old enough to remember when selling hamburgers was a mom-and-pop business. Like the shoe-shine trade is today. If I told you I was going to become a multimillionaire in the shoe-shine business, you'd probably think I was nuts."

"I'd have to see it to believe it," was the politest reply Len could think of.

"The interesting thing is that if in 1950 I had told you I was going to be a multimillionaire by going into the hamburger business, you would have thought me nuts, too. Yet fast food has become a big moneymaker.

"Even today, the real success stories in fast food are about people who are known in the industry as 'restaurant people.' People who go into the business just because they see it as an opportunity to make money never seem to make as much money as 'restaurant people' do from a fast-food franchise. And what does the industry mean by a 'restaurant person'? Simply individuals who believe that the food business is fun. They enjoy creating food that customers like and they love serving customers. For them, making money is a bonus.

"The grocery industry is another example," Richard continued. "In 1945 there were lots of corner grocery stores, but by 1955 many of these small family-run operations had their backs to the wall. The big supermarkets were driving them under. Only a madman would have set out to make his fortune in the small grocery store business under those conditions. Yet today, convenience food stores are a big industry with good profits.

"I once met a man at a convention who runs one of these chains, and I can assure you he loved that business and was having fun. He gave me a ride back to the hotel, and it took us over an hour to make the ten-mile trip because he stopped at four of his stores on the way.

"The company had installed new tabletop coolers that allowed each store to display fruits out in the open while at the same time keeping them fresh. Every time he saw an orange or a melon picked off one of the new cooler tables, he would literally hop up and down with pleasure. Today, convenience stores like his serve a multimillion-dollar market. They seem a far cry from the old-fashioned corner store, but they're essentially the same business.

"The point is that hamburgers and corner food stores once looked like mundane run-of-the-mill businesses with no future, and yet they became big success stories."

Len wanted to believe Richard's contention that if you were having fun and also met the other two requirements that Roberta Bains and Carlos Grover would teach him, almost any business could be a big moneymaker. It sounded great, but Len thought it was perhaps too simple to be true.

Len began by asking questions about businesses that suddenly went bankrupt because the market they served changed overnight. He also asked about instant-success stories, people who fortunately latch on to a new fad. It was tough for Len to believe that having fun was going to make much difference to making it big or going broke in those situations.

"What you are talking about is luck," Richard shot back. "I can tell you one thing about luck. People who pass the three tests of making money don't have much bad luck, they have lots of good luck. If you want to try making money with luck only, I suppose it happens. Just as once in a while someone breaks the bank at Las Vegas or wins the lottery.

"One trouble with luck, aside from sitting and waiting around for the lightning to strike, is that sometimes people who do happen on a lucky streak think they know what they're doing. Next thing you know, they're broke because instead of understanding that they were lucky and cashing in their chips, they think they're smart and keep going. You see it in the real-estate business and in the stock market all the time. A wise Wall Street investor who invests hundreds of millions for pension funds once warned me:

Never Confuse Brains with a Bull Market

"The secrets of making money you're going to learn from us," continued Richard, "may not be the only way to become rich, but the nice thing is that you control them and they work. I believe they'll work for anyone prepared to believe in them and use them. Now shall we continue or do you want to put your trust in luck?"

Len could see that Richard didn't have much time for those not ready to believe in the test of joy, so he quickly assured Richard he wanted to continue.

"I've never thought myself lucky, so I'd best go with fun, although I'd never have believed before I walked in here this morning that fun could make money. Nor that the fun had to come first."

"I know it's tough to believe, but if you're going to make big bucks, I've got to convince you of two things: The secrets are more important than the kind of business you're in, and the fun has to come first. If you'd prefer to be playing golf during your business day rather than playing at the office, you can forget about making money. Unless, of course, you'd like to trust in luck, but I don't advise it. I'd rather go with a proven success," said Richard, looking directly at Len.

"I think there's another alternative," ventured Len.

"How's that?" asked Richard, giving him a puzzled look.

"Well, if you love golf, you could go into the golf business."

"Right you are," Richard exclaimed with delight. "Just so long as you don't trust in luck."

Len thought for a moment, then wrote down:

Love Thy Business
or Try Las Vegas

He showed the pad to Richard.

"I think you understand." Richard laughed.

"What if you like the business but don't love it?" questioned Len. "I'm excited about the work I do, but I'm not having the kind of fun you're talking about. How can that be?"

"That's a good question," replied Richard. "I've told you how to meet the test of joy: You can't make money unless you're having fun. Why don't you think about your question overnight. Let's have breakfast in the morning and see what you've figured out. Do you know Don's Cafe on the West Highway?"

Len did.

"Fine. Let's meet there at eight. They have a great breakfast special."

Richard waved a cheery good-bye as he settled himself once again behind his unique desk.

❖   ❖   ❖

That night Len made a list of everything he had learned:

1.   You can't make money unless you are having fun.

2.   When you're having fun, work becomes play.

3.   The fun has to come first. Then success follows.

4.   Any business can make money if you know the secrets of making money.

5.   People who know the secrets of making money naturally enjoy good luck.

6.   If you don't love the business, you may as well try Las Vegas if you want to make big bucks.

This all made sense to Len, but the next morning as he stood shaving at the bathroom mirror, he was still puzzled as to why he liked his job, but wasn't experiencing the kind of fun Richard was talking about.

Walking downstairs a few minutes later he was startled by the slam of the front door. His wife stood at the foot of the stairs, a wet newspaper in hand and an annoyed look on her face. The paperboy, rather than putting the paper up on the dry porch, had tossed it on the bottom step, still wet from the previous night's rain.

"That new paperboy is no good," she exclaimed. "He's only interested in how fast he can finish his route. He doesn't seem to care if our paper gets wet. I'd complain, but his mother is in my church group. Every time I see her she tells me how much he enjoys the paper route and what fun he's having seeing how fast he can finish delivering his papers. I haven't the heart to complain."

"I've got it," Len exclaimed with glee as he picked up his wife and hugged her.

"Got what?" she asked, startled.

Len took out his notebook and pen. "Just a minute and I'll show you," he said.

He thought for a moment, then wrote:

Business Takes Place
When the Customer Uses the Product

His wife took a look and suggested that if that was a stroke of genius, it was well disguised.

"The paperboy is having fun with a delivery system," Len told his wife. "But he really doesn't care about our reading the paper. His fun is directed at the wrong thing."

His wife looked as puzzled as before.

Len promised to explain later. Right then he was off to see Richard.

When Len arrived at the restaurant Richard was already at a table. Don's Cafe wasn't as fancy as Len's usual breakfast spot, but he could see from the food on the adjacent tables that it was probably a better place to eat, and there was no doubt it was a much better deal. It didn't quite fit the elegant, elder-statesman image he had of Richard, but then neither did Richard's office. Moneymakers, Len thought as he walked over to the table, were a quirky lot of individualists. One label couldn't fit them all.

Once Len was seated, Richard asked him if he had discovered why he was excited about the work he did but wasn't having the kind of fun Richard talked about. Len smiled and showed him his notebook: Business takes place when the customer uses the product.

"The way I see it, Richard, is that all of the examples you gave me yesterday were people who loved the product first and the systems for delivering or making the product second. They only valued the systems to the extent that the systems helped the product serve the customer. The systems as systems were not their first love.

"I'm a good manager and I enjoy my job, but what I like are the systems and making things work in the department. I don't think I really care much about our company's product. If tomorrow we were to suddenly change our product, the only interest I'd have is how it would affect the way we do things in my department and what adjustments I'd have to make. I think I like the systems for themselves. Not because they add value to our product for our customers or even because they help someone else in our organization. I just enjoy the systems."

"That's very good," said Richard. "The only suggestion I'd make is a small but important change to the saying you wrote in your notebook. I think it should read: Successful business takes place when the customer *enjoys* using the product. Your wife might have read the wet paper, but she wouldn't have enjoyed it. Joyful customers are raving fans and are willing to spread the good word about your company."

"That's interesting," said Len. "So when you talk about having fun and loving the business, you mean you have to love having the customer not only use the product but feel good about it. That's what has to be fun. The systems for making or delivering the product should be fun not because they are great systems, but because they contribute to the customer's enjoyable use of the product."

"My boy, I think you understand," said Richard with a touch of pride. "Now let's eat breakfast."

After ordering, Len told Richard he had two problems with the test of joy being the key to making money. First, he knew of one very successful moneymaker who was considered a mean person.

"If you are looking for a world-class grouch, this guy would be perfect."

"And the second problem?" prompted Richard.

"The second is my friend Peter. Peter has a decorating store and he fits to a tee your description of loving the business and having fun. I can't imagine anyone enjoying himself more at work. He's never made much money, though. Matter of fact, some months are pretty thin for him. If fun is so important, how can a grouch do so well and a guy like Peter not do well at all?" asked Len.

"I want to believe, but thinking about Peter and this grouch makes it tough."

Richard paused for a moment and then replied, "I'll deal with your first problem. Ask Roberta Bains the second one. You'll be seeing her next, and you're nearly ready to face the test of purpose. But as to your first problem, let me ask you, What makes you think your grouch isn't having fun?"

Richard's question surprised Len. He had never thought in terms of grumpy people having fun.

Richard went on, "I suspect your grouch was having fun and confused work with play. I'm sure he'd be more successful with a better attitude, but in his own way I bet he loves the business. When you're passionately involved, when the issue before you has all of your energy focused, and when you are doing it for some reason other than necessity—that's what I call fun.

"Nowhere is it written that you have to have a smile on your face to have fun."

"You know," replied Len after a thoughtful pause, "you're right. This guy wasn't very happy-looking, but he sure was intense. And he must have been doing it for love. He didn't need the money. In his own way he was probably enjoying himself."

Richard nodded and said, "Before I pass you on to Roberta and let her deal with your question about Peter, I want to be sure I've been clear about meeting the first test."

Taking his pen and a napkin, Richard printed out: YOU CAN'T MAKE MONEY UNLESS YOU'RE HAVING FUN.

"I trust you're comfortable with this idea and believe the power of having fun when it comes to making money," said Richard as he looked up at Len expectantly.

"Aside from my concern about Peter, I'm a believer, Richard."

"Fine," said Richard. "I'll sum it up for you in a short formula."

He turned the napkin over and wrote:

FUN *Provides Commitment and Intensity*
COMMITMENT *and* **INTENSITY** *Mean Focus*
FOCUS *Leads to Success*
SUCCESS *Means Making Money*

Len read this over. "Let's see if I've got it. You're saying moneymakers—those people who make the cash register go *ka-ching, ka-ching, ka-ching*—have a tunnel-vision focus on the customer's enjoyment of their product or service. This focus comes from a real love of the business. So much so that work is enjoyable and becomes play."

Richard gave Len a warm smile.

"You've got it. If you can continue to believe what you've just said and understand that fun has to come first, you are well on your way. The big thing is having fun, which means being really turned on when a customer enjoys using your product or service."

Richard stopped talking and looked at his watch.

"Timing's perfect," he said. "You're due to meet Roberta in half an hour."

THE TEST OF PURPOSE

While driving to Roberta's office Len thought about his last few minutes with Richard. Having checked up on the three people who would be teaching him how to make money, Len had learned something about Richard's business before their meeting. Richard ran what Len thought of as a soap distribution business. Chemicals, cleaning compounds, that sort of thing. But Len had discovered that, for Richard, cleaning wasn't that sort of thing. It was *the* thing.

At breakfast Len had noticed Richard studying an ugly stain on the floor by the restaurant's front door. Richard kept looking at it and mentioned it several times while they ate. On the way out he asked Don, the owner, if he knew what had happened. Don said he didn't know. It had just appeared one day. They had tried everything they could think of to remove the stain with no success.

After getting down on his knees to have a closer look, Richard volunteered to send Don a special cleaning fluid he was sure would remove the stain.

"I like dirt," Richard had said by way of explanation as he stood up and dusted off his knees.

"So I see," Len had replied.

That picture of Richard, down on his knees in an expensive suit delightedly looking at a stain as if it were a crown jewel, would, Len was sure, forever drive home the message of the "fun" secret to meeting the test of joy.

Richard's final words still echoed: "You need to discover what you love, Len."

Len pulled his car into Roberta Bains's parking lot thinking it was easier to understand her passion. Roberta owned and ran a large nursing agency that provided special-care nurses for children in 14 different states.

As he walked into her office, Len took a quick check of the desk. Polished mahogany. Large. Leather high-backed executive chair behind. Nothing like Richard's.

Nor was Roberta anything like Richard. She was short, of a width his mother called pleasantly plump, and, at 34, was exactly half Richard's age. In her pale-blue pantsuit nurses uniform she looked as perfect as Richard in his tailored suit. She also matched Richard's smile and welcome.

"Delighted to meet you. You're Rabbi Silver's find, I hear. I just got off the phone with Richard. I hear you two got on famously. Richard can come off as difficult to get to know," said Roberta, scarcely pausing for breath. "But he isn't really. He's wonderful, but I was terrified when I first met him. I mean the man's a legend, and here I am a pediatric nurse, for heaven's sake. I still do two shifts a week, you know."

"I've read that," said Len.

"Richard told me your question about your friend Peter. Let's sit down and discuss it," said Roberta, motioning Len to a chair.

"Peter puzzles me when I try to fit him into what I learned from Richard about the test of joy," said Len.

"I think the best way to answer your question is to tell you the secret to passing the test of purpose."

"Great," responded Len as Roberta reached into a uniform pocket and pulled out a white card that looked like an exact clone of the one Richard carried. Roberta turned the card toward Len. Looking down at the top half he read:

The Test of Purpose

**You Can't Make Money
Unless Making Money Is
MORE IMPORTANT
Than Having Fun**

"Richard just told me having fun was the most important secret," said Len, peeved and definitely puzzled.

Roberta suggested that Len read it again and think about what it might mean.

After a moment Roberta said, "Think of it this way. If you want to be a champion parachute jumper, the most important thing is to like jumping out of airplanes. Right?"

"I'd go along with that," agreed Len. "You're not going to win any championships unless you jump, and you'd better be happy about it, too. I imagine being pushed and then being terrified wouldn't win a championship."

"Right," said Roberta. "When you think about it, though, just floating through space with a smile on your face isn't going to work very well either. At least not if you want to jump again. Once you're out of the plane you need a purpose, a goal beyond enjoying the plunge. Yanking the rip cord would likely be a good one. And if you want to be a champion sky diver, you'll have to put every drop of passion and energy you have into perfecting your technique. That requires jump after jump after jump. First, you have to exit the plane, but once you're out the door, getting the chute open and practicing technique has to have top priority."

"I've never been skydiving," said Len, "but I can see what you mean. The fun, the excitement of jumping would have to come first, and then once you're plunging down you can still enjoy the ride but you'd need to have opening the chute and guiding yourself to a safe landing as the priority all right. Otherwise it would be a short career."

Roberta laughed and said, "Right you are. The bottom line is if you want to win a sports championship, it would be dumb to go after it in skydiving if you didn't enjoy jumping out of airplanes, but just enjoying the jump isn't going to do it for you. Jumping technique has to be more important than floating in midair."

"Hey," said Len, "I've got it."

Roberta smiled at Len's enthusiasm.

"You're giving me another 'How.' "

"Another 'How'?" Roberta asked, surprised.

"It's just like the first secret. Lots of people know you have to work hard to make big money, but no one ever says how you do it. The first secret tells how. I learned that having fun was the motivating force that gives the energy and intensity necessary for success. The next question is: 'How do you convert the fun to moneymaking?'

"With the second secret, you're saying once you are having fun you have to focus on making money. Unless you're putting yourself in a position to make money and making it is the top priority, it won't happen. Right, Roberta?"

"Sounds good to me," said Roberta. "The thing to understand is that when making money bumps into having fun, then making money has to take top billing. That's the difference between a hobby and a business. If yanking the rip cord dampens the fun of hurtling down through the air, so be it. You'd best put fun second and pull the cord. The same is true in business. It's important that people enjoy their work and have fun, but if that's their main purpose—having fun—the business will never be successful."

Len looked at the card again: YOU CAN'T MAKE MONEY UNLESS MAKING MONEY IS MORE IMPORTANT THAN HAVING FUN.

"The fact is," said Roberta, "there are a lot of people who say they want to make money, but they don't really take making money seriously. They're not willing to make it *the* priority of their business career. They may try to make up for it by putting in long hours and that might help up to a point, but making really big bucks comes only from having a sharp money focus."

Len leaned back in his chair and said, "That's the answer to my question about Peter, isn't it? He always talks about wanting to make money. During a bad month he's really serious about it, but as soon as sales pick up he'd rather have fun than make money.

"I've seen him spend hours helping a customer choose one $40 roll of wallpaper because he's interested in the design problem. I guess you could say he's having fun jumping out of the plane, but he's heading for a splat. And even if he doesn't crash, he certainly isn't going to win any championships."

Roberta smiled. "Richard and I suspected that it was Peter's failing the test of purpose that was the answer to your problem. The business world is full of people having fun at work who say they want to make money but aren't willing to make it the top priority.

"Until intensity, which comes from fun, is matched with moneymaking as a top priority, you don't have the drive—or the right goal—to be a successful moneymaker. And at work that means the cash register won't be going *ka-ching, ka-ching, ka-ching.*

"Remember," insisted Roberta, "the fun of making money is more important than the fun of doing business."

"That's good," said Len. Taking out his pen, he wrote:

The FUN of Making Money
Is More Important
Than the FUN of Doing Business

"I think I like that better than what you've got on your card."

"Okay by me." Roberta chuckled. "But the important thing is that once you understand the message, you believe in it totally and absolutely."

"I believe," replied Len. "But wouldn't it make more sense to switch the first and second tests? Since making money needs to be a higher priority than having fun, why not put it first? Then we wouldn't have all this business of the first being the most powerful, but the second being more important than the first."

"You're right . . . and wrong," replied Roberta.

"It would seem simpler, but you probably wouldn't be nearly as successful making money, and here's the reason: If you put money first and fun second, you'll never get the balance right.

"The world is full of people looking for ways and schemes to make money. What you have to understand is they've got it backward. If they don't put the fun first, they'll never tap into its potential. They'll never understand how powerful and necessary it is in providing the intensity and commitment to succeed. It has to be first because fun is what gives the drive to make money a real chance of success," Roberta concluded with a firm edge to her voice.

Len looked apologetic for having raised the idea of switching the tests, and still puzzled as well, so Roberta went on to explain further but with a less aggressive tone.

"I can see you're still wondering about this. Think of it as energy and discipline. You mentioned that Richard told you the secret to the test of joy made that test the most powerful one. It's powerful because of the energy it releases, but the energy is only maximized when you put it first. Once you've achieved the necessary energy by having fun, it has to be disciplined and directed. That's what the second secret is about.

"Too many people think the discipline and direction have to come first in order to make money. That is how they get off on the wrong foot. Trying to add excitement, energy, and commitment to a primary focus of discipline and direction is darn near hopeless.

"If you're going to be a big moneymaker, you have to get the energy up front. Fun is a time priority. Making money is a strategic priority," Roberta concluded.

"I hear you loud and clear. Energy one, focus two," said Len.

A buzzer sounded from somewhere near the door in Roberta's office. She had warned Len she was expecting an important call. As she excused herself to pick up the phone in another office, she suggested that Len think about the first two tests.

As Len thought more about passing the first two tests, he realized that the secrets fit all of the moneymakers he had researched. Before meeting Rabbi Silver he'd had an idea that moneymakers must have something in common, and so he'd gone to the public library to discover what he could about history's most famous ones.

It had seemed like a good idea, but it wasn't very helpful. The big moneymakers were a diverse lot, and Len hadn't been able to find a common thread. Now he had two, and he was sure that once he discovered the secret to passing the test of creativity he would have a third.

So far it all seemed to boil down to one word: focus.

Focus made possible by the enjoyment and excitement derived from the business itself and making money.

Sitting in the quiet of Roberta's office, Len began to understand what made moneymakers tick. They seemed to possess some sort of overpowering need that put moneymaking ahead of everything else.

As soon as Roberta returned, he asked her: "Are moneymakers as driven as they seem to be?"

"No doubt about it. Most of them are."

"I'm not sure it sounds very nice!" Len blurted out and immediately regretted his comment as he realized Roberta was describing herself. Before he could apologize Roberta broke in.

"Sometimes you're right. A moneymaker's drive can go so far it becomes immoral. I've seen people with the disease so bad that they mistreat employees and hang customers out to dry just to make an extra buck.

"I don't think this happens often, though. Most moneymakers I know have a keen sense of responsibility to everyone they deal with and the community they live in.

"Besides, you can't stay profitable if you chase away customers or mistreat your employees. If one wants to look for the hard-nut cases, though, they're out there. Some of us are miserly, penny-pinching crooks—no sense denying it!"

"I'm sorry, I didn't mean to suggest you were like that," said Len with embarrassment.

"No offense intended, none taken," said Roberta. "Anytime you've got a person with drive—be it for sports, making money, or whatever—you've got the potential for trouble. The thing to understand is that having a goal and being driven by a dream isn't bad. Letting it grow to the point that it's the only thing in your life, that's when you get in trouble. That's why I think it's important that you also have a significance sponsor. Father Murphy constantly puts success in perspective for me, as I know Rabbi Silver will for you."

"Where does the drive for moneymakers like you and Richard come from?" wondered Len.

"There are lots of different things that motivate moneymakers," replied Roberta. "For some, money is a way to keep score, and they like to win. I know one person whose sole motivation is that his father said he'd never amount to anything. It's his way of proving his father wrong. Some people had it hard as children and are determined that their kids won't have to go through what they did. Some want money to help others.

"When I was learning the secrets of making money," continued Roberta, "a very successful gentleman told me his motivation was the 'stark-raving terror of poverty.' He said no matter how much money you might have, if you were infected with the stark-raving terror of poverty, you would always worry about how you were going to feed your family and pay your bills."

"Even if you have lots of money?" asked Len.

"Yup. Even if you have megabucks. Big moneymakers don't define 'lots' the same way other people do. You've met some people who don't worry about money, right?"

"Sure. There's Peter just for starters—except, of course, when he's in financial trouble."

Roberta got up from her chair and walked over to the window. After a few moments she said, "Tell me, what do you think Peter would say about your financial situation?"

"Well," replied Len, "I know exactly what he'd say. He's told me how he envies my regular paycheck. Every time his business is in trouble he tells me how lucky I am to be on easy street."

"And how do you feel?" asked Roberta.

"When I look at the people I went to school with, I know that I'm doing better than many of them. To that extent I'm happy with the money I'm making. But when I look at our bills and the cost of things today, I know I want to make a lot more," said Len.

"You might think it strange that anyone with my money would also worry about having enough," said Roberta. "But I discovered when I started to make big bucks that the definition of what was enough kept moving out further. Not because I was spending a lot more as I earned a lot more. It was because no matter how much I saved or earned I was never satisfied that I was financially secure.

"I'm not struck with the stark-raving terror of poverty the way some moneymakers are, but I recognize that it's part of my motivation. Part of the drive that keeps me going. To the extent it drives me, I don't think it is much different from the way you view your own salary. You probably look at the money I make and wonder how could I worry—just the way Peter looks at you."

Len nodded his understanding.

"Before I turn you over to Carlos Grover for the test of creativity, there's one more thing I want to discuss. I told you making money is more important than having fun. I want to be sure you realize that this means you have to be willing to make tough decisions.

"That doesn't mean you have to be ruthless or unpleasant, but it does mean that for the good of the business you sometimes have to take actions that aren't popular. That call I took. I was letting the head of one of my branch offices in New Jersey know that she wouldn't be the new vice president here at headquarters. I've decided to go outside the organization. I don't often do that. I've got some very good people with me, but this time I need a truly excellent person, and the internal candidates don't measure up to that standard for this particular job. I'm not going to be popular, but it's the right decision. It wouldn't be fair to put her into a job she couldn't handle, and it wouldn't be fair to everyone else in the company or the children who are our patients and their parents who count on us. If you can't face up to tough decisions, Len, you'll never be wealthy."

Len thought this over for a moment.

"I can see why the secret to the second test answers my question about Peter. His focus isn't really on making money except when he's in financial difficulty, and he obviously isn't willing to make tough decisions. He cares, but not enough. While you were out I was thinking it all really hinges on an intense focus. You might even call it obsession."

Roberta walked back from the window and sat down.

"That's it exactly. Except I like the word 'focus' better. Obsession tells you how exclusive the focus has to be, but that's only while you're actually involved with making money. The trouble with the word 'obsession' is that I don't want to lead you into thinking that your whole life has to be focused on moneymaking. It's true you have to commit your business life to it. But this doesn't mean you have to renounce everything else in life and do only business. It doesn't even mean that there isn't room in your business life for lots of things aside from moneymaking. As a matter of fact, I suspect the biggest financial reward comes to those who lead a balanced life."

"It's our old friend significance," smiled Len.

"That's for sure," said Roberta. "But paying attention to significance doesn't mean you turn your back on success either."

Len sat quietly while he considered everything he had learned.

"It's a lot tougher than I thought it would be," said Len. "When I started to read about moneymakers and wondered if they had a common secret, I figured that if I could identify it, I could easily apply it to my own life. The two tests you and Richard have told me about have secrets to passing them that are easy to learn but difficult to apply.

"What you're really saying, Roberta, is that it has to come from within me. I've got to have that drive."

"That's right," said Roberta. "You now know how to pass the first two tests, and after you learn the third, you'll have everything you need to make big money. Whether or not you do it, though, depends on your own commitment and drive."

Len realized that Roberta was talking about a lifetime dedication—to put making money out front as *the* priority of his business life.

"You look a little stunned," said Roberta.

"I guess I am," agreed Len. "I'd always figured that someday I could be a big moneymaker. But now, after what you've told me, I doubt I've got the kind of commitment it takes to do it."

"Do you feel as if I've killed your hope of making big money?" asked Roberta.

"I guess so. Even though I know I might never make it, I always thought I had a chance. Now I'm not so sure."

"You're forgetting something," said Roberta as she once again slid the white card across the table toward Len.

Looking down, Len saw what Richard had shown him:

The Test of Joy

**You Can't Make Money
Unless You're Having
FUN**

"Remember what Richard told you. The fun has to come first."

Protesting, Len replied, "But you've just told me that I have to be focused on and even fascinated with moneymaking in my business life. I don't know if I've got that kind of commitment."

"You're forgetting the 'How' of the first secret," said Roberta. "I'm sure Richard gave you the formula earlier:

FUN Provides Commitment and Intensity
COMMITMENT and INTENSITY Mean Focus
FOCUS Leads to Success
SUCCESS Means Making Money

"Here you are not even having fun yet and already you're worried about commitment and intensity. First you have to be having fun."

Len wasn't at all happy with this reply.

"With all due respect, Roberta, you still haven't answered my question. What if I'm having fun and don't have the will to put making money before the fun of doing business?"

"The answer to that's easy," said Roberta. "Unless making money comes first, you won't make much. But I wouldn't worry too much about that if I were you."

Len waited for Roberta to continue, but she just sat and looked at Len while Len stared back.

"I can give you the answer," Roberta said at last. "However, it would be better if you can at least get a glimpse of it on your own. We're talking about a critical point, and if you can grab on to the answer yourself, you'll remember it much better than if I tell you the whole thing. So, please, take your time and think about it."

The conversation stopped while Len reviewed in his mind everything he had covered with Richard and Roberta that morning.

First: When Richard talked of having fun in business, he meant enjoying the customer's feeling good about using the product or service.

Second: You didn't have to have a smile on your face to be having fun. Fun, Richard said, was when you were passionately involved, focusing your energy and doing it for a reason other than necessity.

Third: Fun provides the commitment and intensity that adds up to focus, which leads to success and making money.

Fourth: You can't make money unless making money is more important than having fun—or, as Len preferred, the fun of making money has to be more important than the fun of doing business.

Fifth: Peter didn't make any money to speak of because while he might be having fun in his business, making money wasn't a top priority.

Sixth: All moneymakers have something that motivates them. Some are even infected with what Roberta called the stark-raving terror of poverty.

Seventh: Roberta said the most . . .

"Hey!" Len burst out. "It's a question of motivation, like proving your dad wrong or the stark-raving terror of poverty, isn't it? If you've got motivation of some sort, you will put making money before having fun, and if you don't, you won't."

"Right on!" exclaimed Roberta. "As far as I'm concerned, there are only two kinds of people in the world. Those who at some point have enough money and then are glad to take the rest of their lives off to smell the flowers full-time and those who never have enough money because they're motivated to make more.

"It's the same with business. If you're having fun in a business and can pass the other two tests, I believe the amount of money you make will be within a few dollars of the point you define as enough.

"But either personal or business, if you reach a point where you think you have enough money, you'll stop striving to make more. If you're truly infected with the stark-raving terror of poverty, or if you're determined to eradicate poverty in inner-city slums or have a burning passion to increase shareholder value or whatever, you'll never stop."

Len thought this over. Obviously he hadn't even come close to making what he considered enough money. Now if he could just develop the fun attitude Richard spoke of, perhaps his future would be bright after all. Then his face clouded over.

"One thing bothers me, Roberta," said Len. "I'm worried I'm going to open a Pandora's box with fun and focus. I don't want to get carried away and always be doing business. I want to be wealthy. I'm willing to adopt fun and focus, but I'm afraid if I do what you and Richard suggest, I'll wind up a workaholic, never home, miss the children growing up, cell phone on the golf course. . . ."

"That's a valid concern," said Roberta. "The answer is that you need to become a peak performer, not a workaholic."

"And the difference is?"

"Peak performers are able to shut the motor down and focus on things other than work. That's why peak performers not only lead a better life than workaholics, they're also more productive."

"I can see all that," said Len. "The workaholic would be burning out while the peak performer was recharging. So how do I avoid burnout and find a way to recharge?"

"Excellent question. I can give you a couple of guidelines. First, like significance, you have to be intentional about it. You have to schedule downtime to see your child's school play or watch soccer practice. And you have to stick to it. Then you need to pay more attention to Rabbi Silver when he talks to you about significance than you do to Richard and me or Carlos when we talk to you about making money. You won't find and achieve significance if you're a workaholic."

"Is it the difference between being obsessed and being focused that we were just talking about?" asked Len.

"That's right."

After a moment Len said, "With fun and focus, becoming a workaholic is a risk all right, but I'm aware of the danger and I'll keep close to Rabbi Silver. What's next?"

"Next, you tell me what your motivation to make big bucks really is," said Roberta.

"I'm not sure. I guess I'll have to discover my motivation," said Len thoughtfully.

"That's right," said Roberta. "You need to be clear about that. When the going gets tough, you'll want to reach out to your motivation for energy.

"I know I'm motivated by several things, but my core motivation is never to worry about money again. I grew up in a home where some days I went to school hungry. I never want that to happen to my children. When I need energy, I think of that and I get fired up. I may have enough to feed them, but I don't have enough to feed all hungry children. I give generously to children's causes and it drives me.

"In my company the drive we all share is a little different. First, we're committed to increasing profits so that our sharing program for team members gets bigger every year. Second, we're committed to increasing shareholder value. Finally, we're clear about how we're going to do it. Excellence in nursing care for our patients is our overarching goal. The better we get at that, the more profitable we are."

Then Roberta looked Len square in the eye and said, "You need to know your motivation, Len. Both for yourself and for your department at work. Sit quietly for thirty minutes every day with a pad and pencil. Write down every reason you can think of. When you hit the right one, you'll know instantly. I suggest once you discover it, you write it down and pin up copies of it wherever you can."

"I'll do that," promised Len.

"You've got a while till you're due to meet with Carlos Grover, and I think you know how to pass the test of purpose. May I treat you to lunch?"

"I'd love that," said Len as images of posh dining rooms at exclusive country clubs swirled through his head.

"Do you happen to know Don's Cafe out on the highway? Great burgers," said Roberta brightly.

"Matter of fact I do," said Len. "Great breakfasts, too!"

"Tell you what," said Roberta. "We've got a whole fleet of drivers and shuttle buses moving our nurses from assignment to assignment. I'll have them take your car over to Carlos's, then we can ride together. Carlos wants to meet you at the ballpark. I'll drop you off there after lunch."

"I'd like that," said Len, handing her his keys.

"Cheeseburger, fries, hold the onions, extra pickle, here I come," said Roberta, and off they went.

THE TEST OF CREATIVITY

The stain was gone. Len wondered if Richard had come back and cleaned it up himself.

"What happened to that stain you used to have here?" he asked Don, pointing to the clean floor. "Looked like a bad one to me and it's vanished."

"If I'd known it was this popular I'd have made it a monument," said Don. "You're the second person in here today who wants to talk about my stain. Twenty-three years in business no one cares about my stains. Is this national stain week or something?"

"Not that I know of." Len smiled. "I just wondered what happened to it, that's all."

"Gone," said Don. "Guy in here this morning fell in love with it. Two hours later a crew of three he sent show up, and ten minutes later it's gone. If I'd known you wanted to see it, I'd have kept it. You want I should spill something for you on the floor, or are you here for lunch?"

Len was amazed to hear what Richard had done, but not surprised.

"I really think you're going to make a lot of money," said Roberta once they were seated and had ordered their burgers. "You've got what it takes."

"How's that?"

"Well, most moneymakers are, how shall I say this, a tad eccentric. Richard has his plywood desk. I wear my nurse's uniform to work even when I'm not nursing, which some think is a little strange for the CEO of a multimillion-dollar company. You come into a restaurant and start a conversation with the owner about stains he used to have on his floor," said Roberta, giving Len a look somewhere between curiosity and respect.

"You're a weird one, Len. You and I are going to get along fine. If you ever get tired of Richard as your main sponsor, you let me know."

"My main sponsor?"

"Hasn't anyone told you? Everyone we work with is assigned a success sponsor. You're Richard's man. Just like Rabbi Silver is your significance sponsor. You can change, of course, but the idea is to give you someone on the success side of the equation to work with you closely on your moneymaking journey."

Roberta's eyes lit up as a huge cheeseburger was placed in front of her and her attention became totally focused on lunch.

Roberta dropped Len off at the city's new 40,000-seat ballpark, and within minutes of meeting Carlos Grover, Len decided that Carlos too was touched with that independent-minded unusualness that in the very wealthy is known as eccentricity, and among members of other classes as "weird."

"Glad to see you. Glad to see you. Richard's called me twice about you already. Says you're going to be a blessing to all of us. Do us proud," said Carlos, shaking Len's hand with an enthusiasm Len had last encountered when a friend had invited him to a Rotary Club luncheon.

"Sorry I couldn't be with you earlier. Rotary Club today," said Carlos, at which Len decided he could add the honorific "psychic" to "weird."

"Good to meet you," Len managed to squeeze into the conversation before Carlos, who had replaced his handshake with a firm grip on Len's elbow to guide him into the ballpark, started to quiz Len on all he had learned so far. Carlos might be like a walking chamber of commerce pitchman, but his mind was razor-sharp and his questions probing.

"So you've got it all," concluded Carlos as he escorted Len down a ramp marked Player's Entrance. "You're clear, confident, and satisfied it's complete?"

"Well, Carlos, I've still got one problem."

"And that is?"

"I still need more 'How.' Once I'm having fun and determined to make money, just how do I do that?"

"Ah, my friend, now you're talking about meeting the third test," Carlos said with a delighted twinkle in his eyes. "The next 'How' of making money.

"You'll recall Richard told you the first test was the greatest of the three and then Roberta said the second contained an element more important than the first."

"I sure do," replied Len.

"Well, if you miss on this one, the first two are worthless. Rather than show you my copy of the card, I've got a better idea. Follow me."

At the bottom of the ramp Carlos said hello to the guard, then walked Len into the empty ballpark and out onto the dome-covered field.

"I think you'll always remember the secret to meeting the third test, the test of creativity," said Carlos with scant disguised delight as he strode out across home plate to the pitcher's mound.

"ALL READY HERE," boomed a voice over the loudspeaker system. "WAVE WHEN YOU'RE READY, MR. GROVER."

"Watch over there," said Carlos, pointing to the outfield as he raised his arm.

Suddenly the huge ballpark screen came to life in full blazing color. Red rockets with yellow tails blazed across the screen. Golden trumpets replaced rockets as the park reverberated to a military fanfare from unseen loudspeakers.

The screen went blank. "THE SECRET TO MEETING THE THIRD TEST," an announcer's voice thundered, and then it was there. Up on the screen.

Simple black letters on a white background:

The Test of Creativity

Income Less Expenses
Equals
Profit

Len stared at the screen in wonder, waiting for a further message. Soon it became apparent that this was it. INCOME LESS EXPENSES EQUALS PROFIT. Filled with awe at the production, if not the message, Len turned to Carlos and then back to the electronic billboard.

"Wow!" he exclaimed.

"It really is a powerful message, isn't it," agreed Carlos.

"I'm sure it is," said Len. "But the wow was for the presentation. How did you do it?"

"That was easy," said Carlos. "At least it's easy when you own the ballpark. But tell me, what do you think of the secret to meeting the test of creativity?"

Len turned back to the electronic billboard. The message began to pulse in time to the music playing on the public-address system. INCOME LESS EXPENSES EQUALS PROFIT.

"Well, Carlos, the secrets to meeting the first two tests were somewhat strange when I first looked at them. This one isn't new to me, but I expect there's more to it, because it doesn't fit any usual definition of creativity that I can think of. You've already told me the third secret is the next 'How' of making money, so I'm eager to learn."

"Great," replied Carlos as he led Len off the field and up to a private enclosed box. The steward who looked after the owner's box had set out coffee and rolls. It occurred to Len that moneymaking must burn a lot of calories. It seemed moneymakers rarely missed a chance to eat.

"I decided to make something of a show of this because this test isn't only important, it is also the one most often forgotten," said Carlos.

"The problem is, it's so simple. There really isn't any magic to making money. All you have to do is decide how much you want to make and then put that spread between your income and expenses, and there you are. You start with setting a specific goal."

Len looked at Carlos carefully. It was evident Carlos was perfectly serious. All you had to do to make money was to decide how much you wanted to make and then make that the difference between your income and expenses.

"The secrets to meeting the first two tests have shown me I have a lot to learn when it comes to making money, and I know the three of you are experts," Len said. "So without wanting to sound ungrateful, I've got to tell you this secret is pretty obvious. It's about as helpful as somebody telling me the way to reach a ripe old age is don't die before my 90th birthday."

Carlos looked up from the roll he was buttering, and his face crinkled with glee.

Jabbing with the point of his knife out the window where the secret to meeting the test of creativity still flashed on the scoreboard display, Carlos said, "Well, let's take a look at it. If that's true, what does it tell you?"

"First off, I guess the most important message is that you can only have a profit if your expenses are less than your income," ventured Len.

"True enough, but if you are going to make big money, you've got it backward."

"Backward?"

"Yes, backward. The real story is that if you are going to have a profit, your income has to exceed your expenses."

"Isn't that what I just said?"

"It is and it isn't," replied Carlos. "It all depends where you want to put the emphasis. You can't ignore either side of the equation. The mistake most people make in business is concentrating on the expense side rather than on the revenue side.

"You have to understand, maximum profit is controlled by revenue. Regardless of what you do with expenses, you can never make more than your income. If you want to make big money, you have to create sales. It doesn't matter if you're talking about making money for yourself or for your company, it's producing revenue not squeezing expenses that separates the moneymakers from the also-rans. Moneymakers spend their time on what really matters, and what really matters is creating revenue."

"The test of creativity," said Len with sudden understanding.

"It's embarrassingly obvious, but I never really thought about it quite like that. Our company is always so concerned about keeping expenses under control that I never stopped to think the best we can do—even if we had no expenses—is make 100 percent of our income."

"Right," replied Carlos. "Now don't get the idea that expense control isn't important. It is. But it really isn't the key to profitability."

"I think the president of our company would drop dead if he heard you say that." Len laughed.

"I don't doubt it," said Carlos, "and he doesn't make very much money either. I took the trouble of checking up a bit on your company. I was able to get your financial statements for last year, the year before, and the first two quarters of this year, and I can see he isn't a big moneymaker."

Len's first thought was that there really was an information network open to moneymakers and not known to the rest of the world. His company's financial statements were closely guarded information.

Len's second thought was that the idea that expense control wasn't the key to profitability still seemed close to heresy.

Len voiced his concern: "Isn't it dangerous to be the head of a company and go around saying expense control isn't the key to profitability?"

"Dynamite," agreed Carlos. "It can be a recipe for disaster. People can get careless with expenses. But if you are going to make big bucks, everyone in the company has to eat, sleep, and breathe income. Expense control is a great idea and you can be in big trouble if you let expenses get out of hand, but the secret of making money is making it—not squeezing it once you've got it in your hand.

"I remember the first job I ever had. I was sitting at my desk when the owner stuck his head in the door, looked at me working away, and in a half-sad, half-disgusted tone of voice said, 'I suppose you're trying to figure out how to make money?'

"I should tell you this man was getting on in years but was still sharp as a tack and a legend in our town as a moneymaker. I told him that was exactly what I was doing—going over the next month's budget to see if there was anything we could cut. Instead of praising me, he shook his head sadly and muttered, 'You really don't understand, do you?'

"I must have looked pretty upset, so he tried to make me feel better by saying, 'Look, it isn't your fault God made you dumb. You just don't understand. Look at me. I'm a multimillionaire, and all my life all I ever tried to do was to keep the cash register ringing.

" 'Day in and day out I kept that cash register going *ka-ching, ka-ching, ka-ching,* and I discovered that as more money went through the register more turned into profit.'

"Now this man didn't spend a dime if nine cents would do, but the great lesson he was teaching me was that you make money by creating sales, not by pinching pennies."

Len smiled at the thought of Carlos trying to impress his boss and having his balloon popped so quickly.

"If controlling expenses isn't the key to making big money, how come managers spend so much time worrying about it?" asked Len.

"Good question. I'd be glad to tell you what I've decided about that, but first, wouldn't you really rather ask me why expense control is second to sales?"

"Just the question I wanted to ask."

"I hoped it might be," Carlos deadpanned, "because it just happens to be the question I'd like to answer."

Carlos looked down longingly at the remaining rolls before giving into temptation and having a second one. "I skipped dessert at Rotary," Carlos explained.

"It took me a while to understand about expenses. The value of expense control is vastly overrated. Well, perhaps that's an overstatement when so many organizations seem to be so inefficient, but expense-control obsession can lead you into a blind alley. It becomes an activity of quickly diminishing returns with no upside.

"First, say it takes six months to trim 10 percent off costs. To improve from 10 to 11 percent might take another six months. To go to 12 percent, perhaps an extra year or more. Soon the return on your time isn't worth it. You have to keep a constant vigil on expenses, of course, but it can't be your main focus or even a major item of management time.

"Second, very soon you begin to cut into the fun. And once you do that the business begins to die.

"When managers step in and trim expenses, they are second-guessing the people they manage. They're doing what their people should be doing rather than setting those people up for success. If the payoff is trimming a reasonable percentage from expenses, people respect you. If you continue to second-guess them by looking for an extra percent, or a fraction of a percent, they'll very quickly stop taking risks and trying new things.

"The energy that they should be using to build the business goes into making sure they don't make a mistake, and they focus on covering up in case they do.

"Obsessive expense control by management is the embalming fluid of business."

"Hey, that's a great line," said Len as he reached for his notebook to record it.

"Glad you like it. I sort of fancy it myself," said Carlos with a smile. "Expense control, like embalming, lends a fiction of life to a company that may already be dead, and if it isn't, it soon will be.

"But there is more," continued Carlos. "Not only do your people turn off, but soon sales support and customer service begin to fall to the axe as well. Cut too much and sales go down. It gets you both coming and going.

"Richard told you about his Wall Street investor friend who taught him not to confuse brains with a bull market?"

"He did," said Len.

"Good. Well, here's a bit of wisdom I learned from an investor friend of mine."

Taking a pen and paper from his pocket, Carlos printed out a message and then turned it toward Len.

You Can't Cost-Cut
Your Way to Prosperity

"While we're on expenses and sayings, here's one of my own I think you'll like," said an obviously pleased Carlos as he recited aloud:

Cost Control
Will Keep You Whole,
but for Profits to Soar
It's Big Sales You Must Score

Suddenly Len's face lit up.

"I've got it, Carlos. Listen!

"You're telling me most people have expense control all wrong. Managers use expense control to increase profit, but the real importance of expense control isn't to make money, it's to keep you competitive in the marketplace. If costs are in line, it's going to be tough to drive you out of business. That's the importance of cost control. It's bankruptcy insurance," said Len.

"Well, I don't know if it's all the insurance you need, but you've got the message," replied Carlos. "You need to understand that even the media-star moneymakers who are always on the cover of financial magazines and praised for their cost-cutting are far more focused on sales than the journalists understand or give them credit for. And the media stars don't complain. The stock market loves a cost-cutter, and besides, they don't want their competition to get too excited about sales. Better the competition thinks their success is expense-based.

"Now, I think it's time to ask why many managers spend so much time worrying about expenses if sales are more important."

"Consider it asked," said Len.

"You might think I've got some strange ideas, but try this one out," said Carlos.

"I think the reason that managers get it wrong is that cost-cutting is easy. Selling is tough."

"That's a difficult one to wrap my mind around," said Len. "I'll grant you selling is tough, but, I mean, if you're talking tough you're talking hard-nosed, and hard-nosed means Mack the Knife on expenses."

"Who told you that?" asked Carlos. "The best salesman in your company?"

"Of course not," said Len. "I've worked with lots of senior managers, and I know cost-cutting is tough."

"Well, I'm here to tell you that's a lot of bunk," shot back Carlos. "You can cut costs in the comfort of your office, analyzing things you already know well and putting pressure on people who work for you. Coming up with new products is creative. Finding new uses or markets for existing products is creative. Selling is creative. Selling means you have to reach out to people you may not know and then show how you can help them. Convince them they need products or services they are currently doing without.

"Of course, there are true business geniuses who figure out how to really lower a company's cost base. They come up with a way to spend $1 instead of spending $3 and still obtain the same or a better result. My first boss figured out a way to reduce what had been a business that used 12,000 square feet of land, minimum, to one that used 625 square feet maximum with better service, fewer employees, and increased sales to boot.* A true authentic genius.

"But what I'm warning you about are the expense-cutting types who like to pretend they're geniuses. These turkeys nickel-and-dime a company to death. They never talk about the company's product or how to sell it. All they want to do is grind down their suppliers and staff and pretend it's important work."

"You're pretty steamed up," observed Len.

"I guess I am," said Carlos with a sheepish grin.

*You can meet Doug Everett, the man who actually did this, in the acknowledgments at the back of this book.

"Companies are full of obsessive expense-control advocates who are costing millions and maybe billions of dollars in lost profits, and yet no one is pointing out that the emperor has no clothes. Well, it's all a crock!" said Carlos as he dropped back into his chair.

For the sake of Carlos's blood pressure Len decided it would be a good idea to get back to the secret of meeting the test of creativity.

"Earlier on you said the way to make money was to decide how much you wanted to make and then just let that be the difference between income and expenses. That has to be a lot more difficult than you make it out to be."

"Yes and no," said Carlos. "But before I get to that I want to say something more about expenses. I gave you my rhyme: 'Cost control Will Keep You Whole, but for Profits to Soar It's Big Sales You Must Score.' We talked about the importance of sales, but I want to be sure you appreciate how critical it is for the company to keep costs in line. The minute you let costs creep up above those of the competition, you're in real danger.

"I'll give you something else to write in your notebook:

Bad Sales Hurt;
Costs Can Kill

Len leaned back his head and groaned, "I no sooner get a bead on you than you swerve around and come at me from another direction."

"I can be a bit difficult that way," admitted Carlos with a chuckle.

"It's not really new, though. It's just another way of looking at the poetry I gave you earlier. Costs are critical, up to a point. Don't ever forget that. If your costs are out of line, you will be out of business—FAST. But if costs are reasonable, then go for the gold. The gold is creating income and that means bigger sales."

Len, however, was frustrated.

"So if I don't control costs, they're going to kill me, and if I do, it's embalming fluid. No matter what I do it's wrong."

"Don't zero in on the costs. That's not the issue. Look at who is doing the cost-cutting," replied Carlos.

"Come again?" puzzled Len.

"As a manager, your job isn't to do the frontline cost-cutting," said Carlos.

"But a manager can't ignore expenses," protested Len.

"Right you are. But the manager's role is to encourage cost control and set an example. Of course, if the roof is falling in, that's different, but in a healthy, winning company the cost control comes from the bottom up.

"When the guy on the shipping dock gets rid of the fancy sticky labels that cost 15 cents apiece and saves packing material from incoming orders, or when an office worker saves large brown envelopes from the mail to use internally, that's a winning company. The right folks are focusing on controlling costs.

"Top-down cost-cutting doesn't work because as a manager, you don't really know what's going on. You aren't close enough to the action. When it comes from the bottom up it's much more significant—like a shot of oxygen and adrenaline hitting an athlete at the same time.

"Management's cost-cutting role has to be with major cost-base initiatives: dealing with the big things like revamping a whole process or redesigning a product to eliminate manufacturing costs. Frontline cost control belongs with the frontline people. You just have to understand whose job cost control really is," concluded Carlos.

Len's face reflected his pleasure as everything began to fall into place and he understood the logic of what Carlos was saying. "That's what Richard's desk is all about, isn't it?" Len asked. "It's an example!"

"You mean his plywood? It's more than an example," replied Carlos. "It's a statement. At Richard's company they don't waste money. He doesn't waste money. Nobody wastes money. I don't do what Richard does, at least the way he does it. I have a nice desk. But there are other ways I set an example.

"One final thing I need to mention," said Carlos. "It's obvious, but to paraphrase Shakespeare, it's a truth more honored in its breach than its observance. You can never be rich unless you spend less than you earn. Major money may let you spend more, but if you can't keep spending under control when earning minor money, you'll never pull it off earning major money."

"It's got to be easier, though," said Len. "Surely it's easier."

"Being rich is more than a state of mind, Len. It's spending less than you earn. Even if you have buckets of money, if you spend more than you can afford, you're not wealthy. A person earning $40,000 a year and spending $35,000 is far wealthier than someone earning $1 million and spending $1.5 million."

"And that's not in conflict with the creativity of going for income rather than holding the line on expenses?" questioned Len.

"Not at all. The first, going for income, is how you earn significant money to start with. The second, keeping your spending in line, is the difference between rich and poor no matter how much money you have or may be earning."

"Got it," said Len.

"Good. Then let's move on. You were asking about my contention that the way to make money was to decide how much you wanted to make and then just let that amount be the difference between income and expenses."

"Right," said Len. "You make it sound as if it's easy, but you didn't give me the 'How.'"

"It's not that difficult," Carlos said. "Tell me, how did we get a man on the moon?"

"Rockets?" Len ventured.

"Fiddle," said Carlos. "President Kennedy was frustrated when the Russians beat us into space, so he declared a specific goal: The United States would put a man on the moon and return him to earth safely by the end of the decade. The point is, you can't do it unless you decide to do it and really mean it.

"The very act of making the commitment is often the 'How.' It can still be tough, but with the decision clearly made, nine times out of ten it will all fall into place."

"You mean if I want to make a million dollars all I have to do is decide I really want to make a million dollars?" Len asked dubiously.

"I mean you will never make a million unless you decide to make a million, and deciding and meaning it is just as tough as doing it," replied Carlos.

"Let's go back to Kennedy. Getting a man into space, much less to the moon, was incredible. Tell me what would have happened if Kennedy had simply set putting a man in orbit around the earth as his goal?"

"I guess we would have had a man in orbit instead of on the moon," replied Len.

"Too right," Carlos retorted, banging his cup on the table for emphasis and startling Len in the process.

Carlos, however, continued without missing a beat. "Goal-setting was critical to the moon-walk success. If you're going for the moon, you have to shoot for it," he observed. And it didn't much matter if it was sales or rockets.

"Now you're going to say, 'That's fine, but how am I actually going to reach those sales dollars?' But you see, the problem will be easier to solve once you really make up your mind to do it. There is a big difference between trying to figure out how to do something if you want to and how to do it if you have to."

"But . . ." Len hesitated. "Can it really be such a big difference?"

"You're darn tootin' it's a big difference," said Carlos. "Before the decision to make $1 million, the kind of questions to ask are:

What is a reasonable profit target?

What are the problems?

Who can do it?

How long will it take?

Can the company afford it?

Will the competition allow it?

Is plant capacity available?

Can we train the new people needed?

Etc., etc.

"After the decision is made, all that is down the toilet. Those questions are irrelevant. The question now is how, not can, and there is a world of difference. All of a sudden people are asking, 'How do we hit the profit target?' instead of what a reasonable target might be. And 'How do we solve this problem?' rather than wondering what the problems are.

"You'd be surprised how creative people can be when they understand the company is going for $1 million, and the ones going along will be those who answer the 'How' question. It's not the threat of being replaced that motivates people. At least not the good ones, the ones you want. It's the excitement of going for the goal, having the chance to be part of the success, that gets them going."

Carlos fell silent and Len looked out from Carlos's private box across the ballpark to where INCOME LESS EXPENSES EQUALS PROFIT continued to pulse on the screen.

When he'd first seen the message Len had thought its meaning was obvious. Now he saw the secret to meeting the test of creativity through new eyes:

- He understood that it was income that limited profits.

- He saw expenses in a new light. Lowering the cost base in a major way was an important job for management, but frontline cost control was best left to the front line. Further, controlling expenses was the key to protecting the company from being put out of business by a lower-cost producer, but not the answer to making big profits.

- He realized that to make money you first had to decide how much money and then make a commitment to that goal a reality, a reality that was definitely going to happen as sure as the sun would rise in the morning.

- And finally, Carlos said that it would be much easier to solve the problem of how to boost income once a firm commitment to do so was made.

These same principles could also guide his own quest to make big money for himself.

Out on the field, the groundskeepers were finishing up their work and members of the home team, in town for a doubleheader, were trotting out for practice. Under any other circumstances Len would have been delighted to watch, but today he barely noticed the activity as he pondered Carlos's ideas.

After a few minutes of silence, Carlos spoke up. "You're wondering how this can be so simple?" asked Carlos.

Len nodded.

"The answer is the incredible power of goal-setting," said Carlos. "By goal-setting I don't mean a wish list. I'm talking about making up your mind so firmly and being so committed that the goal is a reality for you before it actually happens. That's power goal-setting.

"Prior to making the decision of how much money you want to make, the focus of your energy is on the problems, difficulties, and risks of such a commitment. When you think about how you might reach the goal, your mind works on the question of how difficult it would be, so you can plug that into your risk/reward analysis.

"The more you study the question, the more the risks become evident and the rewards become hidden.

"Now, I'm not saying to go off half-cocked, but when making a goal decision you need to assure yourself that the risks are not overwhelming and then get going. There will always be risks. The only risk-free environment comes when you're dead.

"Once you make a firm decision to do it—to make the money—you undergo a fundamental change. Prior to the decision, you're busy questioning your *skill* power. After the decision is made, your *will* power takes over and that can be dynamite.

"The magic in the whole thing is the power you have after making the decision. Once you're committed to the goal, your energy is focused on achieving that goal. And the best part is that there is a real clarity to your thinking once you know what you want."

Carlos fell silent as he too watched the players on the field. Then he continued, "Making a goal decision frees the mind to see solutions and answers instead of risks. It isn't thinking that clears the mind. It's making decisions."

Len smiled to himself as a picture popped into his mind of his high school chemistry teacher holding a beaker of cloudy fluid, adding a few drops of chemical, and the liquid clearing.

"One of the main reasons you have to first set a goal is that until you do, you won't have all the information available on how to get there."

"Excuse me?" interrupted Len. "I'm not sure I heard that right. Are you saying that setting a goal somehow creates information on how to achieve that goal? Information that wasn't there before?"

"Not exactly," said Carlos. "But you're close. The information is always there, but until you set the goal, you can't see it clearly. Your senses may be able to pick up the information, but it isn't getting through to your conscious mind."

"I find that difficult to grasp," said Len. "You mean if I want to increase sales, information on how to do that is somehow hidden until I set a goal to increase sales?"

"Until you reach a real decision and are committed to achieving that goal, yes, that's true," said Carlos.

"Our brains block out information that either isn't important or needed for immediate use. Once you set a goal, that information becomes more important and you see it."

"And this is scientific fact?" asked Len with evident skepticism.

"Cross my heart," said Carlos. "Think of a fish. Why doesn't a fish drown? Because it has a monitoring system that takes from the water what it needs and leaves what it doesn't. People are drowning in information, so they need their own monitoring systems to let through the information they need and filter out the information that is unnecessary to accomplish their goals. I don't know how a fish's monitoring system works, but for humans it's well documented. It's called the Reticular Activating Device—or simply RAD. Part of the brain's central cortex, I believe. It's an area that acts as a filter. You can learn more by looking it up in any good book on how the brain works.

"Your mind is continually flooded with information. Your conscious mind can only handle so much of it, so you have to have a filter that blocks out unimportant information."

"And it really works?" asked a still wondering Len.

"You bet," said Carlos. "I guarantee if you decide to buy a new car, the Reticular Activating Device will open up and start to let your conscious mind become aware of information on new cars. The amount of new car advertising will astound you. Every time you read a paper or watch TV information about cars will jump out at you.

"The point is that information is often right there in front of us, but we shut it out unless it is of value or needed right then. The example that many textbooks use is of a mother who sleeps soundly as a train goes by, but when her baby rolls over and coughs, she is instantly awake. My son tells me he and his wife share equally the responsibility for my granddaughter. I'll believe that when I hear they both wake up at night with the baby. Fact is, she wakes up and that son of mine sleeps so soundly his wife says the world could end and he'd sleep through it all."

Len said it was a great example. His wife had always accused him of ignoring the children during the night. "But one time when she was away, I woke up every time they made a noise. Then the first night my wife was back home I slept like a log again, and I never heard a thing."

"You heard all right," said Carlos. "Your RAD just short-circuited the information when your wife returned. When you needed to know, it let the children's noise through, otherwise it filtered it out.

"That's also why the 'How' often becomes obvious when you really need it. Once you make a decision, your mind becomes focused on where you are going. All of a sudden you can see the route.

"Before the decision, risk information is critical and has a higher priority. After the decision, information on how to increase sales becomes critical and is allowed into the conscious," concluded Carlos.

Len's head shot up as if he'd been jabbed.

"It's like the wilderness trip I went on last summer. We had to climb rocks and rappel down cliffs with a rope. The whole point was to show us what we could do if we actually had to do it.

I remember standing at the bottom of a 75-foot cliff they expected us to climb. It was sheer rock. There was no way I was going up there. Any sane person could see it was impossible.

"Then one of the guides tied on a safety rope, walked up to the wall, and with fingernails and toe tips began this human fly act.

"Next thing I knew this woman, her name was Carrie Anderson, says she'll give it a try. Understand, Carrie is no great athlete or anything. Twenty minutes later she's on top. Then my wife went up. I decided if she could do it, I had to try.

"On went the safety belt and I was amazed as I started to climb how many little crevices and handholds there were on the rock. Once I was under way I could see above me where I was going next. 'Climbing with your eyes,' the guide called it.

"Most amazing of all, I found myself going to the top using footholds that weren't much more than scratches on the rock face. Let me tell you, bumps on the rock that were either ludicrously small or couldn't be seen at all before I started up began to look real good when I was 50 feet high and clinging. When you can't go back down, almost anything can be used to get to the top. And I didn't slip or need the safety rope once," said Len, still thrilled at the memory of what he had done.

"It wasn't easy but it wasn't half as tough as I thought it would be."

"Another great story," enthused Carlos. "It covers everything. First, the decision to go was tougher than the actual climb. Second, before you decided to go it seemed impossible, but once you decided—really decided—you soon saw a way of doing it. Tell me, once you started up, could you see more than one way to the top?"

Len replied that there had been options. "For the most part, one choice looked better than the others, but several times there were equal alternatives, so I'd try to look beyond to see what might be ahead. All the way to the top I tried to see my next move."

"Isn't it interesting how simply making a decision lets you see how to do it?" Carlos asked.

"You're right about that," said Len. "As long as I was assessing the risk/reward ratio I couldn't see anything but sheer rock. I mean, smooth and flat. And you're right about making a decision. Before Carrie went up I really wanted to climb, but I couldn't bring myself to actually try it. However, when Carrie did it, and my wife announced she was going too, I wasn't about to be left behind."

"Better to be dead in a messy macho heap at the bottom than alive as a wimp?" Carlos laughed.

"That's it exactly," agreed Len.

"Once I began, I saw all kinds of opportunities— ways to reach the top—that I didn't see before."

"That leads to the third point of your story," said Carlos. "Opportunities, as you call them, that couldn't be seen or were dismissed as ridiculous during your risk/reward evaluation not only started to look pretty good once you decided to go, but were actually used by you to get to the top."

"Right you are, Carlos," said Len. "I couldn't even see an inch-wide ripple just three inches long on the rock face when I was standing at the bottom wondering how to climb that cliff. Once I started up, I was delighted to find that even smaller toeholds worked fine."

Carlos got up from the table, glanced out the window, and suggested to Len that they head back to the parking lot by way of the playing field to say hello to the team.

Back outside the ballpark, the sun, no longer filtered by the huge dome, shone brightly, but Len didn't notice the change as he puzzled over the secret to meeting the test of creativity.

"I can understand the frustrations of people trying to get a fix on making a firm commitment before knowing exactly how it's going to work," he said to Carlos as they walked toward the car park.

"I can just imagine myself at that wilderness rock cliff trying to convince people that once they decide to climb they will find toeholds they can't see from the ground."

"Some people never make big money because they take crazy risks," said Carlos. "Most fail because they don't take any risks at all."

"Speaking of seeing things, my car is supposed to be here somewhere," said Len as he looked around.

"Oops! Forgot to tell you. I asked Roberta to have your car left at a friend's place," said Carlos. "I want you to meet him. Hop in my car. I'll take you over."

"There's one other aspect of Income Less Expenses Equals Profit we need to examine, and that is the question of time," said Carlos as he drove out of the lot.

"Time is an essential part of this formula. Profits are measured in both dollars and time. There is a big difference between profits of $100,000 a month or $100,000 a year. If you are going to make big bucks, you have to have a real sense of urgency. I'm always amazed at the people who understand money leverage but not time leverage. To make big money, though, sometimes it is more important to lever time than money."

Carlos nosed his car out onto the freeway and accelerated into the lane, heading north toward his office. At the second exit, however, he passed the office turnoff to the east and continued on as the road swung northwest.

"I've tried, but I have real trouble with managing my time," admitted Len.

"It's more than time management," said Carlos.

"To lever time you have to do two things: First, you have to have priorities so that moneymaking tasks are at the top, and second, you have to get going and do it now. Right now.

"Time has to enter into every move you make. Getting done whatever you have to do now and not one hour from now or even ten minutes from now is often the difference between being a winner and an also-ran.

"Successful people may be very different, but they all share two characteristics:

"First, they have a mania about getting important things done.

"Second, they are persistent.

"Now, in regard to the first characteristic, I'm not talking about frantic individuals going in all directions. I'm referring to people who are focused and drive hard to complete their objectives. There are too many people who just can't—or don't—distinguish the difference between what's important and immediate and what's not important and therefore can be dealt with later. They return phone calls that could wait and fuss over piles of not very important paper on their desks.

"If you ask them what they are doing, they'll tell you they are clearing their desks so they can get at their work! Successful people do their real work first and then clean up when time permits. But chances are that when they finish their important work there isn't time enough for most of the unimportant bits and pieces. So those items get tossed in the garbage and at no great loss.

"Imagine. There are legions of people struggling to be successful doing the very work successful people throw out!"

Len laughed. "You're right about that! I've done it myself."

"The second trait is persistence," continued Carlos. "It's equally important. Moneymakers not only know where they are going and push to get there quickly, they are also relentless about getting there. They don't admit to failure; they just keep at it and at it until they win."

MEETING A MONEYMAKER

"Well, here we are," Carlos exclaimed as he drove into a parking lot beside a large industrial building.

"Good morning, Mr. Grover," the receptionist sang out as they entered. "Mr. Parker said you might be over. You're to go right up. I'll let them know you're on the way."

Carlos didn't volunteer any information, and Len was glad to let Carlos run the show. Mr. Parker's secretary met them at the elevator.

"How's Bob today?" inquired Carlos as they walked along the corridor.

"Fish heads! We nearly had fish heads," she replied with fond annoyance. "He found a bag of garbage in some back lane this morning and dragged it up here to see what the recycle ratio was. I caught him just as he was about to dump it on his office floor. Good thing I did. Someone had been fishing and the contents smelled terrible."

So saying, she ushered them into the corner office. Before Len could make any sense of her bizarre story, he had a second shock. The desk! In the middle of the office. A sheet of plywood, nicely stained and finished, supported by plastic soft-drink cases!

"Hello, Bob," Carlos said, striding over to shake hands with the man behind the desk. "I've got someone here I'd like you to meet."

With the introductions came the information that Bob Parker had learned how to meet the three tests of a moneymaker 12 years before, mainly from Carlos Grover. "It was before Pastor Edwards linked up with Father Murphy and Rabbi Silver to start the program you're in," said Carlos.

"So, I'll bet Richard's been filling your ears with stories of how you need to have fun to make money," said Bob.

"He did talk about fun all right," a cautious Len ventured.

"I'll also bet you figured the guy was a kook," said Bob. "Hell, if I wasn't so wealthy after listening to Carlos and following the system he, Richard, and Roberta are teaching you, I'd think they were all kooks, too!"

As far as Len was concerned Bob was the one who looked like a prime candidate for kook of the day.

"Bob's in garbage," said Carlos by way of explanation as he waved his hand around the office.

Len had never seen anything like it. One wall was covered with shelves filled with . . . well, garbage. Empty plastic containers, cereal boxes, beer bottles, broken glass, a rusty flashlight, wire, lightbulbs. Even a stuffed seagull. You name it, it was there.

"All of it's right off our own trucks," said Bob with pride. "We recycle everything you see on those shelves."

"I didn't think recycling paid," said Len, staring with disbelief at the "treasures" Bob kept in his office and wondering how you recycled stuffed seagulls.

"It doesn't pay worth a tinker's damn by itself," agreed Bob. "But it costs over $100 a ton to dump garbage into a landfill around here now. If I can recycle some of that garbage, I can save the tipping fee at the dump on the stuff I recycle, plus I get paid for the recycled material. If I can bale it, sell it, ship it, and my net cost is $80 a ton, I've saved $20. It can really add up over a year. What I get paid for most recycled material isn't great, but the bonus is the money I save in dump fees."

Bob might be a kook, thought Len, but he was a bright one.

"If Carlos is running true to form, he has just started to tell you about the two traits of successful people, and having disposed of leveraging time he's ready to get going on 'persistence,' right?" asked Bob.

"That's it," agreed Len.

"Good, he's got you primed and ready for me. I do the 'persistence' part."

Len looked quizzically at Carlos.

"This is Mr. Persistence," said Carlos. "I'll leave you two to finish off. I'm sure Roberta will have your car outside. After you've taken a couple of days to think over what we've talked about, feel free to call if you have any questions. Regardless, Richard will soon be calling you."

So saying, Carlos was out the door before Len had a chance to say thanks.

Len felt lost. Just moments ago he was secure in the hands of Carlos Grover, one of the most respected men in the state. Now he was in the hands of someone who so far seemed to have two claims to fame: first, a penchant to dump garbage on his office floor, and second, an apparent tenacity of purpose sufficient to have Carlos tag him Mr. Persistence.

Len decided he had best get Bob talking before Bob thought of his precious garbage bag. "You learned about the three tests 12 years ago?" he ventured.

"I did, and now I've got all the money I could ever reasonably need, but I'm still setting some aside for a rainy day," said Bob.

"And is it as easy as Richard, Roberta, and Carlos claim?"

"Anything's easy when you're committed to it and having fun."

"How did you do it?" asked Len.

"Well, when I was young I knew I wanted to make a lot of money, and as Carlos told you I'm pretty focused once my mind's made up. After I finished school I decided that I had to find out what Carlos Grover's secret was. My uncle was the district manager for the sanitation department in the area where Carlos lived, so I went to work with the garbage crew that picked up at his house.

"Once a week I'd make sure the truck was at Carlos's house just as he was leaving for work and I'd be out there hustling garbage from his cans and saying good morning.

"Funny thing was, the rest of the week was great, too. I loved doing the garbage route. I was helping to bring a vital service to people's homes by dealing with the biggest problem facing mankind—what to do with the waste and pollution we all generate.

"One day I worked up my courage, introduced myself, and told Carlos Grover what I wanted. The rest is history. He said he'd be glad to talk to me and I made an appointment to go to his office. What he then told me made sense. I'd already discovered what fun collecting garbage was, so although it was a lot of hard work, it was easy work for me because I was doing what I loved to do."

Len felt it was an odd profession to be enthusiastic about, but he was impressed and said so.

"Tell me," he then asked, "do you get many people like me through here?"

"Carlos brings someone by here every couple of months after they've met with Richard and Roberta," said Bob.

"You're a regular stop?"

"You bet," said Bob. "You're not the first. But you're the first to see the secret to meeting the test of creativity on the ballpark screen. That's a new twist."

"Tell me, have all of these people who have met with Richard, Roberta, and Carlos done as well as you?"

"No," said Bob. "In fact, less than half are really in the money so far."

"How come?" asked Len.

"Several reasons. First is that it takes time. Success doesn't just happen overnight. Then some people get frustrated and quit, and others never find something they love enough to really have fun doing it. But while only some have really made it so far, I bet in the end three-quarters will make big money."

"That's impressive," said Len.

"I agree," said Bob. "But don't forget we're starting with a select group and then there's the tin-ear-and-ten-thumb factor."

"Tin-ear-and-ten-thumb? What's that?"

"That's what Carlos calls it. When I learned the secrets of meeting the three tests from Carlos, I asked him if everybody and anybody could make money just by following the secrets. He said no. Some people were born to play the piano and could even do it without lessons. Millions more could be good players with lessons, but there were always people with tin ears and ten thumbs who would never play worth a darn no matter how much they wanted to or how hard they practiced.

"It's the same with making money. Some are just natural moneymakers, others can do it when they learn the secrets and meet the three tests, but there will always be those with tin ears and ten thumbs who can't make money no matter how hard they try.

"That everyone lives happily ever after only works in fairy tales," said Bob. "But while the secrets may not be foolproof, I think you'll be a wealthy man if you're persistent."

"I take it that's your job. To tell me about persistence," said Len.

"That's it," replied Bob.

"Carlos was impressed that I'd started to collect garbage just so I could meet him. He asked why I was so persistent. I told him 'the story,' and now it's my job to tell 'the story' to those Carlos brings by to meet me."

"I'm all ears," said Len eagerly.

"When I was in high school," Bob said, "I had a summer job with a road construction crew. The foreman handed me a sledgehammer and told me to break a concrete slab apart.

"Well, I bashed away for about ten minutes. Some chips came off, but the slab didn't break. I complained that nothing had happened and told the foreman I wasn't strong enough.

"The foreman, who was a little guy, reached over, took my hammer, and without a word began whacking at the concrete. Because of his size he couldn't swing as hard as I had, but after about 10 blows the slab suddenly broke in two.

"I thanked him for breaking it and I'll never forget his reply: 'You broke it. It just hadn't come apart yet. You'll find it best if you want to break something to keep hitting until it comes apart.'

"After work I started to think about what he'd said. I'd broken it. It just hadn't come apart yet. I decided right then and there that from then on if I wanted to break something, I was going to keep hitting until it came apart. Time after time I see people in business give up at the very time they've finally won because they don't stick around long enough to see it come apart."

Len nodded his head. "That is a good story."

"There's a second part that's just as important," said Bob.

"Right after telling me to keep hitting until it came apart, the foreman added a second piece of advice: 'If it isn't going to break, don't bother hitting it the fourth time.'

"I wasn't exactly sure what he meant by not hitting it the fourth time, but after I'd been on the job for a week or two, just looking at most slabs I could tell if I could break them or not. Others I wasn't sure, but if I put the hammer to them, by the third blow I knew the answer. It was just something about the way the blows felt.

"It was a great lesson and one I've always tried to follow. If I can do something, and provided it's important, I see it through and do it no matter how tough it may be or how long it may take. If I can't do it, I don't waste any time or effort on it. If I'm not sure, I find out as fast as I can—before the fourth blow.

"I've found in life that there are too many people who do all the work of breaking and then don't keep at it until it comes apart. Successful moneymakers are always at it long enough to see it come apart."

"Isn't that a bit contradictory?" asked Len. "On one hand, I'm told moneymakers have priorities and do the important work first, and then you say they disregard time and whack away at something until it's successful."

"Not contradictory at all," replied Bob.

"If you have priorities, the slab you're hitting is the most important one to break, and provided it can be broken, the moneymakers don't stop until they're successful. And Carlos told you about levering time. All the time moneymakers are whacking away, they are constantly looking for ways to lever their time. More efficient, faster ways to deliver the blows. Moneymakers accomplish more than others do in the same amount of time. That's how we become wealthy and also have more time to play golf."

Len saw a chance to get a fresh perspective on something that had been bothering him. "You started by saying, 'provided it can be broken.' Richard claims any business can be a moneymaker if you meet the three tests. I suspect there are businesses that can't be successful. Ones that can't be broken, to use your metaphor."

"I hate to disagree with Richard on anything, and I'm not sure we'd really disagree, but I'd say even if all businesses could be broken, some would take too long to break. That can be a problem. Research on motivation is clear. Achievement-motivated people like goals that are moderately difficult but achievable. People who are not achievement motivated set goals that are either too easy—they can be accomplished with little effort—or too hard—they won't be criticized for not accomplishing them. Since high-achievement-motivated people want goals that will stretch them but are achievable, persistence makes sense to them. Persistence only pays if success is attainable within a reasonable time frame. If it's not, it's like the man said, don't waste your time trying to break it.

"We're not talking about the real problem people actually have, though. The trick is to focus on a money venture where you're having fun first. Not one where you go into the business because you think it's a moneymaking opportunity.

"The next real problem is that people give up too early. Not that they flog a dead horse. That's what I learned breaking rock. That's why I tell you the story."

Len said, "When I first went to see Richard yesterday morning, I thought I'd learn some magic formula. But what you're telling me is there is no magic. Just lots of work that won't be work if I'm having fun. I simply have to get going and keep at it."

"I think I'm supposed to give you another message," said Bob.

"What's that?"

"Well, Carlos never says so, but I think the reason he likes to bring aspiring millionaires up here isn't just so they can hear about persistence."

Len cocked his head and waited for Bob to continue.

"The other reason is to take a good look at me."

"At you?"

"Sure. One look at me and you ought to be saying, 'If he can do it, so can I.'"

"Oh, I'm sure . . ." began Len, but he was cut off by Bob.

"If you're going to be wealthy, you have to face facts, and the fact is I'm a bit of a bumpkin who barely made it through high school, a garbageman to boot, and a multimillionaire. I may not have graduated at the top of my class, but I'm not dumb and you'd have to be very dumb not to get the message that if I can do it, you can, too."

"Some choice." Len laughed. "If I disagree, you've labeled me a dolt, and if I agree, I say you're a bumpkin. I think I get the message."

"I hope you do," Bob replied seriously.

"Everything else isn't worth a tinker's damn unless you understand you can do it. Making a million or two isn't something reserved for anybody in particular. If I can do it, believe me you can, too. Provided you believe you can. You have to believe first."

Having delivered this message, Bob rose, a signal that the meeting was ending.

"As Carlos said, Richard will be calling in a day or two. Take some time to think about what we've told you. Right now, I'll bet the only thing standing between you and making millions is believing you can do it. You know how to meet the three tests."

"Thanks," said Len. "I appreciate the help and your time."

"No problem. If you ever doubt you can make millions, you're welcome to give me a call and we'll have lunch. An hour with this bumpkin will do wonders for your ego."

Some bumpkin, some kook, thought Len as he picked up his keys at the front desk and headed for his car. But he's right. If he can do it, I sure can!

THE WEALTHY EMPLOYEE

Len spent the next two days thinking about what he had learned, so he was glad when Richard telephoned to suggest a meeting. When Len met Richard, he had several questions.

"You've told me about making money for a company," Len plunged in as soon as he and Richard sat down to talk. "But what about making money for myself as an employee?"

"That's tougher," said Richard. "There are three simple rules, though."

"Which are?" prompted Len.

Rule One: *You can't earn a big salary working for an organization that doesn't pay big salaries.*

Rule Two: *You can't earn a big salary working in a job that doesn't carry a big salary.*

Rule Three: *If the company doesn't qualify under rules one and two, move to one that does.*

There was a short silence while Len considered this.

"Well, if nothing else it's to the point," allowed Len.

"It's also darn good advice," said Richard.

"I get fed up listening to people who work for some outfit that pays a middle-of-the-road scale complain about the money they make. When they went to work there the company paid middle-of-the-road and will probably always pay middle-of-the-road. Yet these people carry on as if it's the fault of the company that they don't make big bucks.

"Take public education, for example. I think there is nothing more important than the education of our kids, so I think good teachers ought to be paid big salaries, or at least as much as top-level school administrators. Unfortunately, that's not the case. So if you go into teaching, you must accept the fact that your job will not make you rich."

"But you might be rich inside," said Len. "Teaching can be such gratifying work."

"Absolutely," said Richard. "Teaching can easily pass the test of joy. But teaching isn't a high-income profession. You're never going to be financially rich as a teacher, so stop complaining and blaming the school system. It's a fact of life.

"Now if you're determined to teach and you want to earn more, go ahead and demand more. I wish you luck. But don't be surprised if the system doesn't change just because you want it to.

"It's like going to live in Florida and then starting to complain that it's hot in the summer. If you want cool summers, go live in the mountains, and if you want to earn big bucks, go work for a company willing to pay big bucks."

Len thought this sounded reasonable and was about to say so, but Richard plunged on. "Then there are people who work in low-paying jobs who think they should be paid superstar salaries just because they do a great job. Baseball players get big bucks in this country if they are superstars. Basketball players can rake in the big dough, too. But volleyball players are not really in the money no matter how good they are at the game.

"It takes a 13-year-old kid about two minutes to figure out that if he wants to earn big money at a sport, he'd better sharpen his basket-shooting skills or turn out for batting practice rather than for volleyball, but many full-grown adults can't seem to get that point into their heads."

"So what do you do if you're in a volleyball job?" questioned Len.

"Well, one thing you don't do is earn big bucks, and I'd just as soon you didn't bellyache around me about it," retorted Richard.

"The worst complainers are folks in support roles. Well, maybe they're not the worst, but they're typical. The fact is support folks get a good wage, but they don't get paid like a company superstar—even if they are an accounting, personnel, or purchasing superstar.

"The superstars, who get paid like superstars, are usually the ones closest to the till where the money comes in. I know company presidents who take home less some years than they pay their top salespeople, but they never take home less than the accountant. In certain industries special creative or technical skills are well rewarded.

"If you want to earn a fat-cat salary, you have to find a company that pays fat-cat salaries and then you have to see just which jobs in that organization pay the biggest money and go for them.

"If you're working for an organization that pays big money and you have a big-money job and are really producing for them, then you can complain if you aren't getting paid enough. But don't live in Florida and complain about the heat in the summer."

Len listened to Richard with increasing concern.

"It sounds like what you're telling me is to forget making big money unless I've got my own business."

"That may be a bit of an overstatement," said Richard. "There are lots of big-paying jobs working for someone else. Even then, though, a huge salary isn't going to satisfy you if you want to make really big money.

"You have two choices. First, learn to save your money and invest in businesses you have studied. Or work with an investment advisor or stockbroker you know and trust. Even though my business is successful I've got a sizable account with my broker, Jake Sather, at Peterson Securities. Jake's a genius. We've done very well. I own pieces of several successful businesses, thanks to Jake. One of his other clients I know takes his profit-sharing money from where he works and gives it to Jake to invest. Jake's advice has made him very wealthy. I also know some teachers who have saved money, invested wisely, and built a real nest egg.

"Second, you can start your own business. It's tough, but if you're successful, the returns can be enormous. It's our old friend leverage again."

"How's that?"

"Simple leverage," replied Richard. "Leverage just means you multiply.

"When you leverage time and money you boost earnings, and a company's share value is determined by multiplying those earnings. Leverage a little time or money on the front end, and those share certificates spin upward in value."

"I've seen shares soar when there were no earnings. Matter of fact, one company I can think of had bigger and bigger losses every quarter, and its shares kept going up," challenged Len.

"Short-term public markets can be driven by the Greater Fool Theory," said Richard. "That's the belief that it doesn't matter what you pay because somebody who is a bigger fool than you will come along and pay you more than you paid. That house of cards always comes tumbling down.

"What might be happening, though, is that savvy investors are looking to future earnings and realize current losses are really an investment, like a retailer building market share or an oil company drilling for new reserves that will pay off in the future. Long-term, however, the only thing that determines share value is earnings. Short-term, aside from someone manipulating the stock or a spontaneous outburst of gamblers looking for even greater fools, the only thing that determines share value is earnings or the anticipation of earnings."

"If you can't get stock where you work, if you don't have stock options, I guess you can always invest in your own stock portfolio," said Len.

"Sure," said Richard, "but remember that unless you make investment decisions based on excellent research and knowledge, the stock market is a high-level form of gambling. Either you have to devote the time to this yourself or work with a professional investment counselor. If you don't have equity shares where you work, look for a company with a profit-sharing plan. Some call it gain sharing. You can then leverage that income by investing elsewhere."

Richard didn't leave any doubt about what Len had to do if he wanted to earn more money for himself or about the kind of company he needed to work for if he didn't own his own business. But Richard wasn't finished.

"I want to be sure you understand that you can leave here today and start on the road to making a million dollars if you decide that's what you want to do and believe that you can do it," said Richard.

"I think so," said Len.

"You *think* so!" Richard cried out in anguish. "I've invested a breakfast and all this time in you. Roberta buys you a burger and drives you all the way across town. Carlos puts the secret to the test of creativity up on the screen. Then to top it off he takes you to meet Bob, and after all that, you just *think* you can do it?"

Len's eyes widened, his jaw set, and he actually drew himself up in his chair.

"Thinking has nothing to do with it, sir," he said with formality and a touch of steel in his voice that Richard hadn't heard before.

"I was just trying to sound modest. I not only know how to make money, I know I'm going to do it. As a matter of fact, I've already done it in my mind. Let me show you how."

"Bravo!" cried Richard. "You're really going to go places."

CONFUSION CORNER REVISITED

Len did go places. It didn't happen overnight, but he began to make money as quickly as anyone else his mentors had seen before.

On the fifth anniversary of Len's introduction to the St. Mary's basement Saturday night card game, the priest, the minister, and the rabbi invited Richard to join them and give a report. They'd meet with Len later to hear his own story, but first they wanted to get Richard's perspective.

"Our boy Len is doing well then?" Father Murphy asked as he held his cards out at arm's length and squinted slightly to see what he'd been dealt.

"Huge success," said Richard, "but the real news . . ."

"Tell them about the salary and stock options first," broke in Rabbi Silver. "While I've been his significance sponsor, Richard has also been keeping me informed on the success side."

Richard said, "You'll remember I told you that Len decided he was going to adopt a different attitude toward his job, to consciously enjoy the fun aspect of seeing the customer use the product or service rather than focus only on the systems."

"I do," said Pastor Edwards. "It never ceases to amaze me how that can happen. Take a job, any job. Some hate it, some naturally love it, and some are able to find joy in whatever they do."

The table fell silent while the four laid down their cards and again Father Murphy swept the pennies over to his pile.

"Once Len started to appreciate the value of what his company did for customers and began to view his work through the customers' eyes, work, he told me, just didn't seem like work anymore," said Richard.

"He was confusing work with play," said Rabbi Silver. "Now, tell them about the salary and stock options."

The card game paused as Pastor Edwards and Father Murphy looked expectantly at Richard.

"Well, as Len began to enjoy work and truly got excited about the moment when the customer used and enjoyed the product, his energy and concentration level soared. He got so pumped up that just by listening to him the rest of his department also became enthused. At the end of the first six months expenses were down and productivity was way up," said Richard.

"He then sat down with his boss, showed him what had happened, and laid out his plan for where he was going to take the department. Then he said he didn't want a raise."

"He said what?" exploded Pastor Edward. "Our boy must be crazy!"

"Crazy like a fox," continued Richard. "He said he didn't want a raise in the traditional way. Instead, he wanted a performance bonus and stock options. He told his boss he knew that the company paid superstars well and he wanted to be recognized as one of the superstars. He gave them six months to make up their minds."

"Not bashful, that's for sure," marveled Father Murphy.

"Actually, he was reluctant, but I pushed him hard. He showed me the numbers. He was worth it. He figured his boss would have a fit, but instead the man promised Len he'd go to bat for him. Three months later the top brass decided not only to increase Len's salary but also give him options."

"He made a killing," said Rabbi Silver with such pride you might have thought he was his success coach.

"I wonder if we might interest the lad in tithing?" wondered Pastor Edwards as he gathered the cards and began one of his showy Las Vegas–style shuffles.

"I hope so," said Father Murphy. "Came from a fine Catholic family as I recall."

Rabbi Silver gave Father Murphy a mischievous grin and said, "Did I tell you I've always thought Len would make a great convert to Judaism?"

The priest looked up with mock alarm, but before he could say anything Rabbi Silver laughed. "You're safe. I've been spending all my time on significance, not conversion."

"I can report," said Richard, "that the rabbi has done a good job on significance. I want to get to that right after I finish my success report."

Without fanfare, the card game resumed.

"What other news about Len?" asked Pastor Edwards as he began to deal.

"Some important news," said Richard. "Three years ago Len realized that as much as he loved his job, he loved fishing more. He heard a rumor that Baker Reel and Rod Manufacturing was for sale. Baker was nearly broke. But the good news was that the selling price was low enough so that if Len cashed in all his share options and mortgaged his future to the hilt, he could swing a purchase."

"Baker Reel and Rod? I think I've heard of those people," said Father Murphy.

"You have if you read the papers. They went public about two months ago," said Richard. "The stock has done very well."

"He's a big success then," said Pastor Edwards as he wondered if three sevens was good enough to beat whatever he'd dealt Father Murphy.

"He is now, but I confess that for a while I wondered if he hadn't traded a fantastic job and huge income for bankruptcy. First two years were tough. Real tough. But he just wouldn't admit defeat. He really loves everything about fishing and particularly the chance to make excellent equipment. You should hear him when he gets going on rod flexing or something called an antibacklash drag on the reels he makes."

"So enthusiasm rescued the business?" asked Father Murphy as the thought came to him that the totally worthless cards he held might be a message of some sort.

"Enthusiasm was part of his success all right," said Richard. "But Len also made it clear that Baker Reel and Rod was finished with the old game of losing money on every sale and making it up on the volume."

"Old business joke," Father Murphy explained to no one in particular as he eyed the three replacement cards Pastor Edwards was flicking his way.

"Not a joke to Baker, I can tell you," said Richard. "They were doing crazy deals under pressure from the big discount stores. Len said thanks but no thanks. He lost two-thirds of the volume he was doing with those mass merchandisers but managed to triple profits in that segment of the market.

"The other big thing he did was to keep his costs in line and focus his energy on creating income. The last owners of Baker had been cost-obsessed and kept beating up on the staff. Len installed monthly department budgets, set by the departments themselves. They were reasonably free to set what expenses they wanted, but then Len held their feet to the fire to never ever go over budget. After department people took control, expenses were actually better than when they'd had a budget imposed on them from the top. The money also got spent where it was really needed, not where some person not directly connected with the department decreed."

"Ah! Grandmother is whispering in my angel's ear," said Father Murphy. He had picked up his cards and now had a pair of tens. He may not have been superstitious, but if there was a message in the new cards at least it wasn't a bad one.

"Pay him no mind," Rabbi Silver advised Richard. "It's just his grandmother-and-angel act. It means he's either got a great hand or the worst possible cards. You can never tell with Murphy. Must have to do with what mood Grandma is in. Go on with your story."

Father Murphy gave everyone a somewhat embarrassed smile while Richard continued. "Once Len identified his profitable customers, he knew they'd be his best source for new business. He was a fanatic about looking after them. He wanted repeat business from regular customers and he wanted all their business. After his first couple of trade shows he started to pick up new accounts unhappy with their current suppliers. He found that most of these accounts had been happy enough with the competitor's product and even with their prices. Trouble was, these customers didn't feel valued or cared for. Many had actually been treated badly. Rude, insensitive, uncaring, uncommunicative, couldn't care less were all words and phrases Len heard about his competitors."

"Sounds like the airline I rode on last month," said Pastor Edwards.

"Or the restaurant where I had dinner the other night," said Rabbi Silver.

"Or the place I'm trying to get my television repaired," said Father Murphy sadly. His pair of tens hadn't been enough to beat Pastor Edwards's three sevens.

"It's not an uncommon experience," said Richard as Pastor Edwards reached out for his winnings. "Len didn't want it to be a Baker Reel and Rod experience, though."

"Easy to say, but how did he do it?" asked Father Murphy.

Richard replied, "He realized he had to surround himself with a team who were also having fun, who also loved fishing and could get excited about the moment the customer used their products. He also had to learn to back off and let his team make some of the decisions. He found that tough to do, at least in the beginning."

"Either Grandma or my angel has deserted me," moaned Father Murphy as he looked at the cards that had been dealt to him this time.

"None too soon," said Rabbi Silver.

"Smart angel," said Pastor Edwards, who, turning to Richard, added, "going after profitable business, budgets, an enthusiastic team. No wonder Len's done well."

"There was a lot more to his moneymaking success than that," replied Richard. "A new banking relationship, redesigned products, an overhaul of his sales force by customer rather than by territory, new packaging, a whole pile of things, but you're right, at the core it was a focus on customer service, increasing sales, budgets, and a gung-ho team that created raving fan customers that made the difference."

"Tell me," said Pastor Edwards, "if Len has come this far in five years, any sign he's ready to go all the way to perpetual prosperity?"

"Pretty soon," said Richard, "because he's a special person. In that regard, I'd like Rabbi Silver to fill us in on the significance issue."

"With pleasure," said Rabbi Silver. "There is no doubt that Len has really focused his business life on making money, but at the same time he's not turned his back on significance. When he discovered that he loved fishing and working in that industry was his 'calling,' he began to get much more interested in his relationship with 'the caller.' Being a believer isn't a precondition to making big bucks, or even achieving significance, but I like to think it helps. Len's made a point of making time for his faith and his family, even when the Rod and Reel business was having a rough time turning around. He's also been a generous contributor to charity and I know he's been really involved with the Nature Conservancy, both as a donor and with its local advisory group."

"Sounds like Len rates well on significance," said Father Murphy.

"He sure does." Rabbi Silver smiled. "I'd be willing to bet he'll make the final leap to perpetual prosperity in the near future. He's just the type to do it."

THE FINAL TEST: PERPETUAL PROSPERITY

Len didn't make the final leap as fast as Richard or the three clergymen thought he might.

An economic downturn that was almost classed as a full-scale recession and a long, slow economic recovery derailed Baker Reel and Rod from its fast climb up the ladder of financial success and delayed Len's readiness to seek perpetual prosperity.

In tough times, Len discovered, people weren't willing to put new fishing gear on their list of things to buy. Once again, Len plunged back into every aspect of day-to-day operations to cheer others on and help wherever he could. He kept his own enthusiasm high so his team, rather than feeling defeat, joined the fight and willingly worked the extra hours and made the extra calls to keep the company afloat. As busy as he was at work, however, Len still remembered significance and made time for his family and the Nature Conservancy.

For four years they slugged it out. In the fifth year, Len's eighth in the fishing business, the market turned and profits came back to levels Len would never have believed possible. Three years later the company stock, which had fallen from a high of $2 to pennies, was nearing $12 a share! At last Len was truly wealthy, and although he wasn't aware of it, he was ready for perpetual prosperity.

As the value of his company increased and his bank account grew to a size beyond anything he had believed would be possible for him, Len noted two things about himself.

First, he remained motivated to make money. In part, the stark-raving terror of poverty syndrome was at work in his life. Despite huge financial reserves and a business now worth millions, Len continued to feel that he needed more money to be really secure. He'd seen several profitable businesses suddenly go bankrupt and he wanted a bigger cushion, particularly after his experience during those bad four years. That was part of it, but it wasn't the only motivation. There were several hundred families depending on Baker, and he felt a huge responsibility to keep the business growing to provide both more security and more opportunity for these people. He didn't realize it, but he was already skating on the edge of perpetual prosperity.

Second . . . well, Len couldn't put his finger on it, but something wasn't quite right.

As he always did when faced with a problem, he went to see Richard or Rabbi Silver. Richard was now nearing 80, but still sharp as a tack. Richard often didn't give Len answers, but he was good at asking the right questions and helping Len discover his own solution to a problem.

Although Richard still went into his office almost every day for a couple of hours, Len knew he liked to get back to his estate in the early afternoons to work in his garden. While hired gardeners looked after the grounds, Richard had a small patch where he insisted on doing all the work himself.

"Helps keep me in touch with God's creation," was his explanation.

Puzzled that although he was now wealthy something in his life didn't seem quite right, Len headed off to visit Richard one Tuesday afternoon.

"I just finished weeding the tomatoes," Richard told him when he arrived. "My back doesn't want to bend over anymore today. Your timing is perfect. Any earlier, you could have helped. Any later, and I'd be napping in my hammock."

"Glad to hear I missed a weeding opportunity," said Len. "But if my timing was perfect, I'd be here at harvest."

"I guess you're right about that." Richard laughed. "I'm going to have so many tomatoes this year I'll be begging friends to take them. How about a walk?"

The two set off in silence down Richard's driveway, enjoying the warm afternoon sun and the expanse of lawn interrupted by groves of trees along the long road to the main highway.

"All well at work?" Richard eventually asked. "Making lots of money?"

"I sure am," enthused Len. "The company is having a record year and so am I. The stock is really doing well, too."

"So, are you enjoying yourself?" asked Richard.

Len shot a surprised look at his host. "How do you always know the right question?"

"Been there myself," said Richard. "Not hard to recognize the signs."

"The thing is, Richard, something doesn't seem right. I'm still having fun at work, but some ingredient is missing. It's as if I'm waiting for something to happen, an emptiness that I don't know how to fill."

"A letdown feeling?" asked Richard.

"Sort of, I guess. But mostly something's missing. I thought that when I had all this money I'd be more satisfied. Somehow more fulfilled. I take a great deal of pride in what I've accomplished on the success side of the ledger. I also am growing spiritually, love my time with my family, enjoy my community work, and I feel good about the money we give to charity. So my significance is on track."

"You're comfortable with the difference between success and significance?" asked Richard.

"I am. I always carry the significance card Rabbi Silver gave me years ago. If I'm waiting in an airport or have a few minutes to kill, I often get it out to have a look."

"I don't think I know that card," said Richard.

"You're kidding. I've never showed it to you? It's great. Have a look," said Len, pulling a card from his wallet and handing it to Richard.

Looking down, Richard read:

Success	vs.	Significance
Wealth	—	Generosity
Achievemnet	—	Service
Status	—	Relationships

"They're contrasts," said Len. "Contrasts in three attributes of success and significance."

"So I see," said Richard. "I've heard Rabbi Silver talk about this, but I've never seen the card before. When I look at the first two, wealth and generosity, I think about people like Sir John Templeton and Warren Buffett. Mega-star moneymakers and enormously generous.

"The second pair, achievement and service, reminds me of Dr. Albert Schweitzer. He achieved great things in his life, but the saying of his I remember is 'This I know. Those among you who will be happy are those who will have sought and learned to serve.'"

"What a great quote," said Len.

"How about Mother Teresa for status and relationships?" asked Richard. "She won more awards and was given more honors than I can count, but her whole life was about creating loving relationships. She valued people as people."

"It's quite a list, isn't it?" said Len. "John Templeton, Warren Buffett, Albert Schweitzer, Mother Teresa. We've pigeonholed them under generosity, service, or relationships, but if you think about it, each belongs under all three."

"I agree," said Richard, handing the card back to Len. "Sounds like you've got a good handle on the difference between success and significance."

"I think I do, too," said Len. "Somehow, though, I feel this problem I have is a significance issue, not a success one."

The two continued to walk for several minutes before Len spoke again.

"When I look at you, Richard, I sense you're at peace with yourself and the world. I want to be just like you. I've always wanted to be like you. I used to think it was the money. If only I had lots of money like you, everything would be great. Now I've got lots of money. Things are good in my life, but they aren't great."

"Was it better before you had big money?" asked Richard.

"I've thought about that and, no, things are certainly better now. Much better. Having the family involved in the business is wonderful and I still want to make more money. Lots more. It's not as if I've now got enough. But I know more money isn't the solution. I think money is part of the answer. It just isn't the whole answer."

Again the two walked on in silence.

"Sounds to me as if you're ready to face the fourth and final test, the test of perpetual prosperity," Richard said at last.

Len stopped dead in his tracks and looked at Richard in astonishment. "The fourth test? But you never told me there were four. Why didn't you tell me this before?"

"There are two reasons we didn't tell you before. First, until now you wouldn't have been ready to meet the fourth test. Second, some people are never ready for the fourth test."

"I don't understand. What do you mean I wasn't ready?"

"Good question. Let me explain," said Richard as he again set off down the drive.

"Let's say you were in the hospital with cancer. I'm the surgeon who can save you. I come to your hospital bed and tell you that the surgery isn't such a big deal. The important thing is to discuss your lifestyle *after* the surgery so that the cancer won't come back. You believe I've got to operate immediately before the cancer spreads, and I tell you I want to spend three days discussing lifestyle issues before I operate. How would you feel?"

"Like it was time to get a new surgeon and fast," said Len.

"No doubt." Richard laughed. "Certainly, you wouldn't be interested in discussing your lifestyle. The fourth test is a bit like that. Things you think are more immediate have to be attended to before you can deal with other important matters. No matter how much Rabbi Silver tried to help you keep success in perspective, until you've made sufficient money the fourth test takes a backseat. And notice I said enough money. For some that may be a few thousand, for others many millions. It isn't the number, it's how happy you are with the number."

"So when can I learn the secret to meeting this . . . this fourth test?"

"I think you're ready," said Richard. "The fourth test is the test of perpetual prosperity. You see, what you've accumulated so far is material riches. What you're missing is true prosperity. Perpetual prosperity. As for when, what about our next Saturday night dinner with Rabbi Silver? That's this week, isn't it?"

Rabbi Silver was no longer senior rabbi. At his urging, a younger man with more energy had been found. By popular demand, though, Rabbi Silver had stayed on. Most evenings he could be found in the synagogue teaching. But on the first Saturday evening of every month he disappeared after sundown to have dinner with his old friends, Len and Richard.

"Here's the secret to meeting the test of perpetual prosperity," said Rabbi Silver right after the trio got settled around the restaurant table four nights later. "Listen closely. I predict these 8 words will change your life.

Perpetual Prosperity
Comes to Those Who
Help Others

"I'll repeat that," said Richard. "Perpetual prosperity comes to those who help others."

"Do what?" asked Len.

"Accomplish their goals," said Richard. "Solve a problem, make a decision, whatever they need to reach their full potential."

"The first three secrets were success secrets," said Len. "I can see this fourth is a significance one."

"You're right on that," said Rabbi Silver. "Moneymaking is about what you can get. Perpetual prosperity is about what you can give. Success at the money level is about what you can achieve. Perpetual prosperity is about how you can serve. There are lots of good reasons to earn money, but some people seek money because of the power and status it will give them to control events and other people. Perpetual prosperity is about loving relationships with other people, not power and control. It's what life's all about.

"People with a spiritual side will tell you that life's about your relationship to God. That relationship is a mirror of the one you have with your fellow human beings, and you can't mess things up with people and expect to be all right with God. While some of us never get beyond money or the things money buys, most of us know there's a void in our lives if we only pay attention to making money."

"And this fourth test is the one that really pays off," added Richard. "Not only in filling that hollow place where something is missing, but strangely enough it can also sometimes pay off in material riches as well."

"Material riches, too?" questioned Len.

"Sometimes," replied Richard. "The first day we met, years ago, I told you that riches aren't a fixed pie that gets divided up with only so much to go around. Riches are created. Primarily by supplying goods and services to others. You add value either to what is already there or you create something new. When you help others realize their full potential, you may well be turning a horse and buggy into a jet plane. The result is a whole new pie of riches, and some of the slices may come back to you."

"Wow," said Len.

"Exactly," said Richard with a chuckle. "When I reach out to help someone else, I often get more back in return. But that is not *why* I help people. That's just how it works sometimes. You don't have to look any further than yourself for proof. I gave you a hand toward achieving your full potential. That opened the door for me to get in on the ground floor of your new business. That was never in my mind. It just happened that way, and as you know the stock is doing very nicely these days."

"But the real payoff," interjected the rabbi, "is that when you help others achieve their full potential, that empty feeling disappears. Helping anyone achieve their full potential . . . Well, it just doesn't get any better."

"I guess my newfound riches are the key to helping others even beyond what I've been doing with significance, but I'm not sure exactly what to do or where to start," said Len.

"First, let's look at what you call your newfound riches," said Rabbi Silver. "Unless you use those riches to help others, you'll never find perpetual prosperity. But your money isn't the real issue. It may allow you to do some good things, but remember, a monk who has taken a vow of poverty can be your equal in helping people. Really helping people is a gift of yourself. Your time. Your energy. Your caring. Your knowledge. Your creativity. It's focusing on giving yourself to meet another's needs, not giving to meet your own needs. Your desire for significance will only be fulfilled when you turn your back on your own needs and truly help others for their sake. That's when, as a manager, you become a servant leader rather than a self-serving leader."

"So attaining and giving away money is only part of the answer?" questioned Len.

"It can help, but as Rabbi Silver said, it isn't the real issue," replied Richard. "Society invented money to give us a common medium of exchange. With money we can look after our basic material needs, but it's an easy and common mistake to think that money can take care of our relationships with people. Money can buy other people's time to do things for us. But that's not a relationship. That's a contract. It isn't what other people do for us that matters. It's what we do for other people that counts."

Len nodded his head. "I always thought having lots of money would be the same as prosperity or wealth. It isn't, though. I now understand that it's just one factor. But you were right. Until I experienced big bucks, I wouldn't have been as open to the secret of the fourth test. Now I see it may be the one that matters the most. I also have a feeling I won't be so dedicated to making money," said Len.

"Sure you will," replied Richard. "But I think you'll find the focus moves from the first three tests to the fourth. Now significance becomes more important than success. Helping others gives meaning and purpose to the first three."

Having finished dessert and paid the bill, the three ambled out of the restaurant to where they had parked their cars. Usually the three shook hands when they parted, but on reaching the parking lot Len stopped and, turning to Richard and the rabbi, opened his arms and spontaneously gave them each a hug. And they both hugged him back. Tonight the hugs came naturally.

"Thanks, Richard. Thanks, Rabbi Silver," said Len, stepping back. "This is truly a wonderful gift you have given me."

"No," said Richard. "It is you who have given us a gift. You've allowed us to help you strive to reach your full potential. That is truly a precious gift. I thank you."

"So do I," said the rabbi.

From that time on Len put the secret of perpetual prosperity to work in his life. Some afternoons he left the office early to spend time on the various community projects with which he was now involved. For as Len prospered, he enjoyed being able to offer even more time and money to help people.

Len was amazed at the many opportunities there were to help others. As Richard had predicted, his material riches assisted sometimes, but the real gift he had to give to others was himself. The more he gave, the fuller his life felt and the more of himself he had to give.

One Saturday Len told Richard and the rabbi that he'd like to write a book to tell others about the same secrets Richard, Roberta, Carlos, and Rabbi Silver had taught him.

"That's a great idea," said Richard with obvious delight. "But you have to promise me one thing."

"Sure, Richard, what?" agreed Len.

"If you mention me, please be sure you spell 'Richard' right."

EDITOR'S NOTE

When the working draft of this book was completed, Len proudly delivered a copy to Richard.

"I trust you'll approve," said Len. "I worked hard to tell the secrets exactly as you, Roberta, and Carlos taught me—and you'll notice I did manage to spell 'Richard' the right way."

"I'll be watching for that," replied Richard. "Now I hate to be rude, but if you'd get out of here I could start reading."

The next day Len received the manuscript back from Richard with several comments penciled in the margin. There was also an envelope. Opening the envelope, Len discovered a short, handwritten note from Richard:

> Well done, my friend, well done. I think
> it's about time I passed this along to you.
> I know you'll treasure it as I have.
> —Richard

Clipped to the note was a dog-eared white card, which had printed on one side:

> *The Test of Joy*
> **You Can't Make Money**
> **Unless You're Having**
> **FUN**

And on the other:

The Test of Purpose
**You Can't Make Money
Unless Making Money Is
MORE IMPORTANT
Than Having Fun**

And:

> *The Test of Creativity*
> **Income Less Expenses**
> **Equals**
> **Profit**

Across the bottom of both sides, he discovered in Richard's handwriting:

The Final Test
**Perpetual Prosperity
Comes to Those Who
Help Others**

GOOSE HONKINGS*

From first draft to final manuscript, this book has been more than 10 years in the writing. During that time many people have read and reread the book as it progressed and have given us great feedback. We are indebted to all. In particular we thank:

Senator Douglas D. Everett, whose wisdom sparked this book to begin with and who actually took a business requiring a minimum of 12,000 square feet and reduced it to 625 square feet with better service, fewer employees, and increased sales to boot!

*Honking geese are cheering each other on according to Andy Longclaw in *Gung Ho!* the second book in our trilogy.

Phil Hodges, the managing director of the Center for Faithwalk Leadership, who has brought balance and perspective to the book, and we thank him for continually challenging us and asking the tough questions.

E. J. "Ted" Ransby, President, GWL Investment Management Ltd., who warned us not to confuse brains with a bull market and taught us that you can't cost-cut your way to prosperity.

Hugh Goldie, of the Exchange Consulting Group, who read the initial manuscript 10 years ago and has been pushing us to completion ever since.

Hon. Richard Spink Bowles, Sheldon's father, who before his death read an early version of the manuscript and gave us wonderful advice, all of which is incorporated into the book.

John Messenger, former headmaster, St. John's Ravenscourt School, who has achieved both success and significance.

As always, we are indebted to **Richard Andison, David Baldner, Sheldon Berney, Trevor Cochrane, Carl Eisbrenner, Derek Johannson, Ray Kives, Richard Kroft, Mel Lazareck, Sam Linhart, Bob May, Michael Nozick, Maureen Prendiville, Hartley Richardson, Ross Robinson, Paul Schimnowski, Harvey Secter, Gary Steiman,** and **Jim Tennant.**

The two teams of support at Ken's and Sheldon's offices, **Eleanor Terndrup, Dottie Hamilt, Kelly DeLuca,** and **Rita Loewen.**

The Gung Ho Team that guides our work: **Michal Yanson** and **Zach Schisgal** of William Morrow, **Dick Lyles** and **Harry Paul** from The Ken Blanchard Companies, and **Margret McBride,** our literary agent. We also extend our thanks and best wishes to **Michael Murphy.**

The following, all of whom have carefully read the manuscript and have provided us with excellent feedback: **Steve Gaudreau**, Power Inc.; **Jake Beard** and **Willie Sather**, Morgan Stanley Dean Witter; **John Peterson**, Paine Webber; **Allen Snart**, Western Management Consultants; **Frank Felicella**, Golf San Antonio; **Ron Hill**, Misericordia Health Center; **David Johnston**, Johnston Group Inc.; **Paul Fazio**, Sonny's Enterprises, Inc.; **Kent McAllister**, Health Midwest; **Richard** and **Susan Silvano**, Career Management International; **Barry Graceman**, 3G Enterprises; **Pam La Palme**, Scotiabank; **Sandra Ford**, The Sandra Ford Agency; **Dave Tucker**, Peco Corporation; **Ian** and **Sandy McLandress**, **Carolyn Ransby,** and **Ed Chornous**; the eight members of the Skaneateles Country Club who joined Ken for a feedback session one evening in August 1999.

We remember the late **Horace Everett**, Canada's largest Ford dealer, who first proclaimed the wisdom that the way to make money was to keep the cash register ringing. We also remember the late **Carrie Anderson** of United Airlines, who scampered up a Colorado Rocky Mountain face and proved that if you're going to the top, foot- and handholds that look impossible from the base look fantastic and work fine when you're halfway up.

We thank **Lou Tice**, The Pacific Institute, who, at a YPO University, first introduced us to the brain's Reticular Activating Device; **David McClellan** for groundbreaking research on Achievement-Motivation; **Charles Garfield** for his insightful studies of the characteristics of peak performers; and **Bob Russell,** senior pastor at Southeast Christian Church in Louisville, Kentucky, and **Bob Buford,** author of *Half-Time,* for what they taught us about the difference between success and significance.

This book is dedicated to the Young President's Organization. YPO was the catalyst that first brought us together, and for 25 plus years has served as a living laboratory for us to study some of the world's most successful moneymakers. In particular we wish to thank former YPO administrators **Gerry Tomas** and **Jill Cochrane,** who first brought Ken to YPO, and YPO'ers **John Anderson, Fred Chaney, Peter Meinig, John Metz, Alan Raffe, Dick Reiter,** and **Red Scott,** who supported him as he made the transition from tenured university professor to business owner and entrepreneur. We also thank **Jim Pattison,** who shepherded Sheldon into YPO, and **John E. Hoegg,** who insisted Sheldon attend the YPO meeting where he met Ken. If it were not for all those YPO'ers' generosity and caring, there would be no *Raving Fans*, no *Gung Ho!*, and now no *Big Bucks!*

Writing a book is always exciting and is made more so by the guidance and mentoring of two of America's finest editors, **Larry Hughes** and **Zach Schisgal**.

In all of our books the most important teaching has pride of place at the end. In *Raving Fans* it was: *Deliver Plus One Percent*. In *Gung Ho!* it was the *Gift of the Goose*: *Cheering each other on*. In *Big Bucks!* it's: *Perpetual Prosperity comes to those who help others*. We end our goose honkings with pride of place at the end to those who are first in our lives: **Margie Blanchard** and **Penny Bowles,** who nurture, inspire, and challenge us. They are both intimately involved in our business and writing careers and we thank them for their love, support, and tough editing, We also extend our thanks to our children and their spouses: **Debbie** and **Humberto Medina, Scott** and **Chris Blanchard, Kingsley Bowles** and **Susan Goldie,** and **Patti** and **Kristjan Backman**. We are blessed to have them as participants in our writing and business lives.

ABOUT THE AUTHORS

KEN BLANCHARD's impact as a writer in the field of management has been far-reaching. The bestselling business book of all time, *The One Minute Manager*® (1982), coauthored with Spencer Johnson, has sold over 9 million copies and has been translated into more than 25 languages. Throughout 1996 *The One Minute Manager*® appeared on the *Business Week* bestseller list along with three of Ken's most recent books, *Raving Fans*®, coauthored with Sheldon Bowles; *Everyone's a Coach*® (1995), coauthored with National Football League legendary coach Don Shula; and *Empowerment Takes More Than a Minute*®, coauthored with Blanchard consulting partners John Carlos and Alan Randolph. No other author has had four books on this prestigious bestselling list in a single year. *The One Minute Manager*®; *Raving Fans*®; *Gung Ho!*® (1998), the second in his trilogy with Sheldon Bowles; and *Leadership by the Book*® (1999), coauthored with well-known minister Bill Hybels and Phil Hodges, continue to appear on the *Business Week* bestseller list.

Ken is Chief Spiritual Officer (CSO) of The Ken Blanchard Companies, a full-service management consulting and training company that he cofounded in 1979 with his wife, Marjorie. The Blanchards are proud of the fact that their daughter, Debbie, and son, Scott, are also active in their businesses. Ken is also a visiting lecturer at his alma mater, Cornell University, where he is a Trustee Emeritus.

The Blanchards are proud grandparents of Kurtis and Kyle, the two wonderful sons of Scott and Chris Blanchard, who live close by in the Blanchards' hometown of San Diego.

SHELDON BOWLES is a successful entrepreneur, *New York Times* and *Business Week* bestselling author, and noted speaker. He began his career as a newspaper reporter and became vice president of Royal Canadian Securities and then president and CEO of Domo Gas. With partner Douglas Everett, Sheldon built that company into one of Canada's largest retail gasoline chains. At a time when competitors were going self-serve, Domo swept to success creating raving fan customers with gung-ho employees. This big bucks success allowed Sheldon to sell his interest and try new, fun things.

After leaving Domo, Sheldon, with three partners, turned a small manufacturing plant into a multimillion-dollar business. Today, in addition to manufacturing, Sheldon has interests in a recycling and waste-hauling business and is hard at work building the finest full-serve car wash in North America. When not pursuing business opportunities Sheldon shares his hard-won knowledge of what works and what doesn't with audiences around the world and in his books, *Raving Fans, Gung Ho!*, and now *Big Bucks!*, all coauthored with Ken Blanchard.

Sheldon, wife, Penny, and their children, Kingsley and Patti, all work with him in business and live in Winnipeg.

SERVICES AVAILABLE

Ken Blanchard and Sheldon Bowles speak to conventions and organizations all over the world. They also have their messages available on audio and video tape.

In addition, The Ken Blanchard Companies conduct seminars and in-depth consulting in the areas of customer service, leadership, team building, performance management, and quality. Sheldon Bowles focuses on customer service and Gung Ho team members.

For further information on Dr. Blanchard's activities and programs contact:

The Ken Blanchard Companies
125 State Place
Escondido, CA 92029
(800) 728-6000 or (760) 489-5005
(760) 489-8407 (fax)
www.kenblanchardcompanies.com

To find out more about having Sheldon Bowles speak to your convention or work with your company, please contact:

Ode to Joy Limited
5-165 Kennedy Street
Winnipeg, MB R3C 1S6
Canada
(204) 943-6642
(204) 947-1536 (fax)

Revolutionize your business with these bestsellers from Ken Blanchard, coauthor of *The One Minute Manager*, and Sheldon Bowles

BIG BUCKS!

NEW!

From the renowned management gurus and *New York Times* bestselling coauthors of *Raving Fans* and *Gung Ho!* comes this simple yet powerful guide for accumulating serious money for yourself and your organization. Packed with practical advice and written in the parable format that made their previous books national bestsellers, *Big Bucks!* is a must-read for anyone seeking to create wealth.

0-688-17035-8

RAVING FANS

Foreword by Harvey Mackay

Just having satisfied customers isn't good enough anymore. If you really want a booming business, you have to create Raving Fans.

This invaluable handbook provides practical, proven advice and innovative techniques that can help everyone in any kind of business deliver stunning customer service and achieve miraculous bottom line results. Written in the parable style of *The One Minute Manager* and using a brilliantly simply and charming story, *Raving Fans* teaches how to define a vision, identifies what a customer really wants, shows how to institute effective systems, and explains how to make Raving Fan Service a constant feature of your business.

"Making your customers Raving Fans is the competitive edge today. This book can jump-start you in that direction."
—James F. Nordstrom, Co-chairman of the Board, Nordstrom, Inc.

0-688-12316-3

GUNG HO!

Bringing the magic of *Raving Fans* to employees, Ken Blanchard and Sheldon Bowles give you foolproof ways to increase productivity by fostering excellent morale in the workplace. This masterful guide reveals the three cornerstones of the breakthrough Gung Ho technique and offers a clear game plan with a step-by-step outline for instituting these simple yet amazingly powerful groundbreaking ideas.

"You need and your business needs *Gung Ho!* This book will revolutionize any organization which adopts it, and those that don't won't survive. It's that simple."
—Tom Peters, coauthor of *In Search of Excellence*

0-688-15428-X

WILLIAM MORROW
An Imprint of HarperCollins*Publishers*

Available in hardcover wherever books are sold, or call 1-800-331-3761 to order.